HERE FOR A GOOD TIME, NOT A LONG TIME

Don't Ignore the Signs

The Tucker Westfall Story

Tracy Westfall

ISBN 979-8-88644-463-6 (Paperback)
ISBN 979-8-88644-464-3 (Digital)

Copyright © 2023 Tracy Westfall
All rights reserved
First Edition

All rights reserved. No part of this publication may be reproduced, distributed, or transmitted in any form or by any means, including photocopying, recording, or other electronic or mechanical methods without the prior written permission of the publisher. For permission requests, solicit the publisher via the address below.

Covenant Books
11661 Hwy 707
Murrells Inlet, SC 29576
www.covenantbooks.com

This book is dedicated to all those who believe
and should believe in the afterlife on earth.

ABOUT THE AUTHOR

Tracy Westfall grew up in a very small rural farming community in Athens, Wisconsin, where everyone knows each other for the most part. She is the middle child of five siblings, having two older sisters and a younger brother and sister. Her parents' families also grew up here, so their family has a long history in this area. Many people in this community tend to remain in the vicinity due to close family ties and a sense of belonging that a small town fosters.

The fact that the events of this story happened in a small town contributed to the impact it had on her, her own family, and on the community as well.

In her late thirties, she had two sons. On June 2, 2018, this mom's worst nightmare came true. This is a remarkable story of one of her sons, a young boy whose life was cut short at the age of fifteen due to a UTV (utility terrain vehicle) accident. Some of the events leading up to that day as well as the happenings after his death are eye-openers to those who believe, for those who want to believe, and to those who should believe that those who leave us here on earth are really not that far away. They are present but in a different soulful form. They hear you, they read what you write, and they love you with an unconditional love, wanting only the best for you. Tracy felt she needed to share her experience with others through this book. Guardian angels do exist. Tracy has one now. It is an incredible story of how her son connected with his mother in a very special way before and after his passing. All she ever had to do was love him, believe he was near, and let him know he could reach out to her. She is here for the rest of her life to be close with Tucker in a much different way than most would ever imagine. Not only is this story interesting, but she wants her story to bring hope to anyone suffering through the grieving pain of losing a loved one.

PROLOGUE

Two opposing high school baseball teams lined up respectively on the first and third baselines. Four umpires ready to call the game stood shoulder to shoulder at home plate. Dirt baselines were meticulously groomed and lined. Grass in the infield sported a fresh cut. The early morning June 14th Wisconsin sky was clear blue with hardly a cloud in sight. There was a very light breeze.

It was a 9:00 AM start for the 2018 WIAA High School Division 4 State Championship baseball game between the Fighting Bluejays of Athens (20–2) versus the Cardinals of Thorp (14–10).

It seemed fitting that the mascots for these teams are the blue jays symbolizing persistence, to fight no matter how hard the situation may seem and the cardinals symbolizing self-empowerment, reaching your goals, and of all good things to come.

There was nervous excitement in the air. Umpires and players removed their caps. Fans in the stands dressed in their respective blue or red attire on each side. Everyone stood up. Hands were respectfully placed over hearts. The outdoor stadium was quiet.

All eyes were focused on the large American flag waving casually out in center field of the Neuroscience Group Field at Fox Cities Stadium in Appleton, Wisconsin. The national anthem started to play. Almost on cue, a majestic bald eagle emerged and soared nonchalantly around the flag as the anthem played on. It was as if it knew all eyes were on him. It had captured the attention of many of the Athens fans and players for good reason. As the *anthem* was ending, the soaring eagle made a final sweep around the back of the baseball field and retreated out of sight.

Hushed comments among the Athens players and fans could be heard—those recognizing the significance of that bald eagle's visit. This was going to be their day. This was going to be their time. Athens knew what was at stake. The team…the coaches…the community wanted this win in the worst way. It was going to be special, and no team they were up against was going to matter. This state baseball title was for the team, for Athens…for Tucker.

CHAPTER 1

In the Beginning

My early years

I grew up a middle child in a small community in Athens, Wisconsin, with four other siblings—three sisters and a brother. My parents grew up in the Athens area as well and only lived a short distance from each other as teenagers. Mom's family had a farm, and Dad's family ran a local bar, where his family lived on the upstairs level. They married in their early twenties. We never had a lot of money growing up but were rich in other ways. Our home was not in the village but located about three miles outside of the village, where my parents still reside. Small farms dot the area, sporting a mixture of old and new farming techniques. Some are Amish families that have moved in over the years. It is not uncommon to see the horse and buggies traveling down the roadsides. I often joke that the biggest traffic jam in Athens is three Amish buggies at the stop sign.

    Mom was a full-time stay-at-home mom, cleaning, cooking, caring for us, and making sure we all got off to church every Sunday. She was a very good seamstress, sewing all of our clothes, even making shoelaces for our winter boots. To earn a few extra dollars, she would waitress in the evenings at a local restaurant and did other interior and exterior painting jobs. Somehow, Mom and Dad always seemed to make ends meet with Dad's income of working at a local co-op, then switching to repairing tractors in a small business operation started by two of my uncles on my mom's side. At times, my parents were down to their last few dollars, but they always managed, getting bills paid, becoming self-sufficient in making necessary repairs on the home, and putting food on the table for breakfast, lunch, and dinner every evening. In looking back, no doubt they were hardworking folks whom I grew to having a great deal of respect for.

This upbringing brought with it a good work ethic, grounded morals and values. I wanted my kids to grow up with this same foundation.

Our family background

My husband, Dale, and I were Athens High School sweethearts in different graduating classes. We were six months apart in age when we started dating at the ages of seventeen and sixteen. Dale attended the Lutheran School, so I did not know him until he entered middle school. I remember first meeting him when a few of his friends were sitting at the top of the bleachers in the high school gym. My interest in boys started about this time, and I had dated a couple of very nice guys. It was awkward, though, like the relationships were fun on a friendly basis, but I was not connecting with them on a "boyfriend" level. My relationship with Dale started out as casual friends. He grew on me with his kindness, cute chuckle, and the way he provided a feeling of comfort. We both enjoyed our sports and each other's company. I remember my history teacher keeping his eyes on us in the hallway between classes. He saw the budding romance and to this day remains a special person in my life. Junior prom held special memories for each of us. I was asked to be on court by a close friend. We went to prom together, and it was about that time that I started to realize just how strong my feelings had grown for Dale. He started to pull at my heartstrings with me wanting to be with him more. The courtship continued. I looked forward to his calls at night, twisting the telephone line around my fingers as we spoke. When he got his driver's license, he'd pick me on Friday and Saturday nights in his red Dodge. What was so unique about that car is that we'd have to lift our butts off the seat before he could turn the ignition on to start it.

Oh, there were a lot of good times in that car. Dale, too, was on prom court his junior year. After the grand march, we attended parties and ended up spending the rest of the evening together. Our love for each other grew. I graduated in 1983, and he in 1984.

After high school, I attended Eau Claire Technical College, Eau Claire, Wisconsin. Following Dale's graduation, he attended the University of La Crosse, La Crosse, Wisconsin. As young adults, we lived in different cities and worked in different places but never lost touch with each other nor our feelings for each other.

Dale graduated from college with a physical education degree and spent over thirty-one years teaching elementary and high school physical education. He was also the head wrestling coach, assistant football coach, and assistant baseball coach, having worked at only two small rural schools throughout these years—Wild Rose School District and Athens School District, both located in Wisconsin. Athens has a population of about 1,000 people, and Wild Rose has roughly 850. Throughout the years, hundreds of parents and kids were touched by his kindness, his ability to interact with students of all ages, and his unique way of using comedy and lightheartedness in how he taught classes and coached. Being a favorite teacher and coach to many, Dale was always finding ways to relate with all students of different ages.

Dale and I dated for seventeen years. Dale finally asked me to marry him at the Paper Valley Hotel in Appleton the day before a Minnesota Viking versus Green Bay Packers football game. This particular day is a little more meaningful than most because of the rivalry that exists between these neighboring teams and how fired up the avid football fans in each state get in anticipation of the game. Viking team players were all over in the hotel, and we were Packer fans. Our families were both very pleased to finally hear the marriage news after such a long courtship (me too!) We were married on *June 6, 1998 (remember this date—it is significant later in this story)*, in an enchanted little outdoor church called the Red Mill located in Waupaca, Wisconsin. It was an intimate, private ceremony in a beautiful setting, followed by a large reception for family and friends. "I Cross My Heart" by George Strait was our song. If you listen to the lyrics, this country music artist sings, "Our love was unconditional, we knew it from the start. In all the world you'll never find a love as true as mine." The song goes on to say we were to share all the love and laughter that a lifetime would allow. I believe we had reached the highest level of love and laughter after having our children. We had it all but are now, to this day, still being tested after losing Tucker. That was the day it started to storm. So now we try to make each tomorrow the best that it can be. It was one of those songs where you didn't know how much of an impression it would have on you until the times really got tough.

Due to my job, it was a requirement that I reside in Stevens Point, Wisconsin. Dale and I purchased a small home in this city and settled in even though that meant Dale commuting forty-five minutes to Wild Rose to teach and coach. It took four years before we were blessed with our first son, Tanner, on May 3, 2002. Tanner was a blond-haired, blue-eyed, small-boned, lightweight child with a quick-learner ability. A year later, our second son, Tucker, was born on May 16, 2003. He was like a baby Dale, chunky in size, heavy-boned, and happy as can be—a very easygoing personality.

Because Dale was a teacher and a coach, there were times when he would go without seeing the boys for days because of his work schedule. Traveling forty-five minutes to work, teaching classes, holding practices, coaching, and attending evening games or matches took its toll on family life. When he did get home late at night, we would briefly discuss the outcome of the game or match, discuss any new developments on the kid side of things that happened before drifting off to sleep. Dale would be up and gone again early the next morning, most days not even having seen the boys. This schedule was not working for him, me, or the kids. There was no family time, and we decided that a change was needed.

Timing is everything. Fortunately, a physical education teaching position opening was posted back in Athens, the very village we grew up in. Dale interviewed for the position and was offered the job. In 2007, we made the move back to Athens. The coach that had coached Dale during his high school baseball years and me during my high school basketball years was now retiring. It was a good time to make this move to be back where our parents still lived, as well as my sisters and my brother. The kids and belongings were packed up, and a white two-story home built in 1891 became our home. It was located within minutes of the school. The house was ramshackled and required a complete remodel. The entire main floor living area was renovated first, then living quarters were switched so the upstairs could be remodeled. While living upstairs, the plumbing was failing, and the electricity was poor with the old knob and tube wiring still in the home. We slept on mattresses on the floor and ate off a card table. Once the main floor living space was done, we were able to live a little more comfortably. The exterior was also completely remodeled with new windows and siding. It now has a beautiful front yard where we spend hours lounging on the front porch, waving to neighbors walking by, watching the neighborhood children on their bikes and people running by, as well as catching the evening sunsets. The open backyard is bordered with large trees with a walking path that leads down to the creek, which can all be enjoyed sitting on the second-story deck.

Tucker's younger years

Upon our move in 2007, Tanner was five years old and starting kindergarten; Tucker was four years old. Both the boys were very well-natured kids. As I stated earlier, Tucker was a heavy-boned boy following in Dad's footsteps. Their baby photos are nearly identical. Tucker was a happy-go-lucky baby, always cheerful and smiling. These traits carried on as he was growing up. His friends enjoyed being around him, and I enjoyed his giving attitude and willingness to lend a hand around the house. He was a bit accident-prone, though. At about age two, Tanner picked up a knickknack and hit Tucker with it above his left eye. No sutures were needed, but there was a small laceration. Years later, Tucker wiped out his bike going around a corner where there was loose gravel near our Athens home. At age eight, he knocked out his two front permanent teeth on the Athens High School gym bleachers when he misstepped and did not catch himself in time. I remember the incident well when he came back down the bleachers and handed me pieces of his teeth. As one would imagine, it was an emergency visit to the dentist. The dentist did a temporary crown, until a year or so later, when he got his beautiful smile back with a permanent crown. And what a beautiful smile he had. No braces needed on this boy.

It was part of my job as a mother to instill good values in my kids. Saying the "please" and "thank yous" and treating elders with respect were important. I could tell if my sons were not telling me the truth (my work training helped me to detect deception), and I'd call the boys out on it if I knew they were not being forthright with me, or I'd asked several questions in different ways. I told Tucker it didn't pay to mislead Mom, and I think he thought I had special powers because I knew when he wasn't telling me the truth. After a few times of being confronted not to lie to Mom (and having his iPhone taken away from him for a period of time), he accepted that somehow I seemed to know, and it was not of any benefit to him. After that, when he got into trouble, he wouldn't keep it from me but felt telling me what happened was the best course, accepting the consequences of his actions and then moving on.

Tucker was a good eater, always enjoying a home-cooked meal. It didn't seem to ever matter what I made, whether it was potatoes, steak, hamburgers, pizza, or spaghetti, he would always eat a good meal and thank me for it as he left the kitchen. I do not recall a time when he did not thank me or comment on how good the meal was even if it was takeout. He was just so appreciative and loved all the little things that mattered so much to me.

Vacations

When the boys got older, every year, shortly after the last day of school for the summer, we headed for some new destination. It was important to us that the boys experience that there is much to see in this world. Their horizons needed to be broadened so they could come to realize that they had choices on where and how they wanted to live.

My older sister, Lorene, and her husband, Tom *(Uncle Tom and Aunt Lorene to the boys)*, were often along on our trips. They live just outside of the Village of Athens and run a very large dairy farm operation called Miltrim Farms. Nearby the farm is where Tucker's accident occurred. Lorene is Tucker's godmother. Both were born in the month of May, so Tucker was a little more connected to her than the other aunts and uncles in our families.

My oldest sister, Wanda, and her husband, Jim *(Uncle Jim and Aunt Wanda)*, would also join in on vacations when they could. They reside in Colorado.

Upon our first travels, we came to learn that Tucker did not do well with traveling, often getting carsick. Dramamine was the remedy that was a quick cure. Our trips were always filled with fun memorable moments, which included fishing, eating, sightseeing, and staying at great hotels and lodges. Our first family vacation was to Florida in 2009. Uncle Tom and Aunt Lorene joined us. In June 2012, it was fly-fishing in Montana and carousing around South Dakota, checking out the Black Hills, Crazy Horse, and Mount Rushmore. In June 2013, we went fishing in the Prairie du Chien area, in southwestern Wisconsin. My younger sister, Georgine *(Aunt Georgine)*, joined us on this trip because we stayed at one of her friend's homes.

In June 2014, the boys and I traveled to Lake Superior for a chartered fishing boat trip. They were so excited knowing they would be sleeping in a boat for the evening before venturing out on the lake in the early morning. The fishing was a success, catching salmon and lake trout. Salmon were fun to catch as they put up quite a fight. That was a special trip as it was just the boys and me.

In June 2015, my fiftieth birthday was celebrated in West Virginia (*"almost heaven"* from "Take Me Home, Country Roads," John Denver's song, a precursor to the future tragic event). Fiftieth birthdays in our family were special. Each of my sisters and brother received a special gift to commemorate their fiftieth. On this trip, the family gave me a gold bracelet engraved with each of my family's names on it… Tracy, Dale, Tanner, and Tucker. Next to each name is our birthstone. I was also presented with a custom-made snapshot photobook of memories starting from my birth to becoming a small girl, to having a boyfriend, to my wedding, and family photos with my sons. It was a most memorable day that I cherish, and we did more fishing! Tucker placed "Take Me Home, Country Roads" on his playlist following our trip.

In June 2016, it was kayaking, fishing, and touring the Jackson Hole, Wyoming area. If I had to rate the trips on scenic beauty, this one is probably the top of my list. Places that we stopped at were some of the most picturesque mountains and waters that I have ever seen.

In June 2017, our travels took us to the international waters in Minnesota, where a large pontoon-style boat was reserved, and the water channels were navigated…and more fish were caught. Grandma and Grandpa Westfall even joined us on this trip. This was our last trip as a family with Tucker. We had planned to go fishing in Minnesota in June 2018, but plans changed; life changed.

Athletic background

Growing up, Tanner and Tucker were best buds one moment and then kicking each other out of their rooms the next. They were typical competitive brothers who were always trying to "one-up" each other or their dad. This competitive nature was a family trait as Dad and I were both athletes in high school. I played volleyball and basketball. Dad was a three-sport athlete playing football, wrestling, and baseball. Dad went on to play college football at UW–La Crosse. The football team won the National Collegiate Athletic Association (NAIA) championship in 1985. He also had a successful high school athletic career, qualifying for the Wisconsin State wrestling tournament and coming in second place at 185 pounds. When the Athens High School baseball team won the state championship in 1982, Dad was a junior on the team. Tucker often eyed up Dad's trophy display case of medals and had his sights set on meeting, or beating, his dad's accomplishments. Setting goals to have more wrestling pins than Dad and wanting to play college football at University of Wisconsin–Madison even if he was a walk-on was on his radar. The red Wisconsin Badgers pair of socks he owned meant much to him, were his favorite, and worn often. Tucker followed the Oregon Ducks football team's success, sporting sweatshirts with their logo during middle school.

Before going out for sports as a high school freshman, one has to pass a physical in order to compete in a sport. The doctor diagnosed Tucker with a hernia. I thought, *How could this happen? How could this be at his age?* Then maybe, I thought, he was trying to get strong too fast, attempting to lift too much weight in the gym. Tucker didn't know when it happened. All he knew was that a hernia surgery would be required before he would be allowed to get on the football field. To Tucker this was like the sky crashing down and the worse news ever. He asked to have the surgery as soon as possible, or he would not be allowed to practice, which meant he would not be allowed to play. Quickly enough, the surgery was scheduled, and the necessary repair was made. I was with him when he went in for the surgery and was there for him during his recovery and discharge. Anxious to get the go-ahead from the doctor, Tucker was cleared and able to play football his freshman year. Crisis averted.

As a freshman, Tucker's body and size was starting to develop, and it looked like he was just starting to follow in Dad's footsteps. Tucker recognized the natural athletic abilities in many of the older athletes at school and was hopeful he could be one of them. His hope and desire was to be on the baseball team that would win a state title once he got old enough to be on the varsity team—just like Dad.

During their younger days, I was the mom who would play catch with boys in the yard. I would drive the boys to flag football games, spend weekends at youth wrestling tournaments and little league games, all in preparation and anticipation of watching them perform in their high school years. Tucker would practice pitching baseballs at a makeshift strike zone box I spray painted on an old door. I leaned it up against an old shed we were planning to renovate, so it didn't matter if the old glass windows got knocked out. Well, Tucker's aim wasn't on with every pitch, so those glass windows were pretty much completely busted out. I'd watch him from my second-story home office window practicing to get his speed and accuracy to improve.

After his freshman year of wrestling, Tucker was not pleased with his performance on the mat, so I pulled out a drawing I sketched of Tucker in 2008, which he had kept in a binder in his room. Mohawk haircuts were in at that age, so in the drawing, Tucker was sporting a mohawk-styled haircut. He was wearing underwear with bulging legs, shoulder, and chest muscles. At the top of the picture, Tucker handwrote, "Tucker in ten years." I placed the binder open to that drawing on his bed and wrote 2018 next to the 2008 date and added a sticky note penciling the following on it, "It takes hard work and dedication, but you can be what you want to achieve." I signed it with a little heart and the word *Mom*. Oftentimes throughout the years, I left notes for the boys and left my signature heart with *Mom* written inside the heart. Once I was certain Tucker had time to digest the note, I knocked and walked in, asking if we could talk. Sitting down next to him while he lay on the bed, we talked about strengths, weaknesses, and goals and how if a person really wants something, that person will need to put forth the effort, and he/she will see the results before you know it. Within days after this conversation, Tucker was working hand crunches while watching TV to strengthen his wrists. I would hear him setting down weights in his room while I watched TV in the living room downstairs. There were other workout noises that I thought were sit-ups and push-ups. I knew then that he had really taken to heart what we talked about and that he wanted to be one of the best, and in order to get there, he would have to work for it. Tucker asked me to take him up to the weight room, which opened at the school every morning at 6:00 a.m. It was really something to see as he would get up on his own in the morning and be ready to go shortly before 6:00 a.m. Tucker got his workout in before classes began for the day. After a short time, the athletic director started picking him up because Tuck was staying on his lifting regimen. The athletic director needed to be up there anyway to open the weight room and drove right by our home to get to the school, so it worked out well. His son was also working out in the mornings, so Tucker had a friend to work out with. Tucker's goal for wrestling was to be sitting in a chair in front of the student body pep rally as one of the wrestlers being honored for qualifying for state.

About this time, I figured I had done all I could. It was up to Tuck to get his body conditioned and learn the ins and outs of each sport to be the best he could be during his high school years in football, wrestling, and baseball. Soon, Coach Dale (Dad) could take over coaching his own son. That was something he desired to do since he had been so busy with his students and athletes over the years that he had not been able to attend as many of the practices, games, and tournaments he would have liked when his own boys were growing up.

During these pre–high school years is when my relationship with Tucker had grown closer, when we had spent a lot of time together traveling to youth wrestling tournaments held on Sundays. It was early to bed on Saturday and up and out early on Sunday to get to the tournaments in time for weigh-ins. After weigh-ins, several hours followed where wrestlers and parents were sitting around, waiting for the mat sheets to get posted to see who the wrestler would wrestle against (usually three other wrestlers of similar weight were in a bracket) before wrestling would begin. Once the wrestling matchups were posted, wrestling was underway with the day ending typically in the early to midafternoon. Upon completion of the round-robin wrestling (wrestling each athlete in their bracket), medals were given out to each wrestler as they took their places on a podium for photos to be taken. Tucker was the guy who wanted photos taken when he won first place in wrestling; otherwise, he wasn't thrilled to have his photo taken. His photographs were often with a tough-looking macho face. In his eyes, it was not cool to smile if you took first. Yet he did not smile either if he had taken anything less than first. As Tucker got older, his athletic photos were always "tough-looking, athletic" expressions. He once told me he practiced facial poses by taking selfies with his cell phone. This way he had experience on how he should look depending on what type of photo was being taken. Following tournaments, a stop to McDonalds was sometimes on Tucker's agenda, with the normal order of a quarter-pound hamburger, six-piece nuggets, and a drink. Never did he alter from that combo order.

Hunting

Our family is also made up of avid hunters, especially deer and bear. My father loves hunting, and so does Dale's dad. It was a part of growing up for both of us and carried through into our boys' blood. One time I recall, at age ten, Tucker and I sat in a ground blind (*concealment shelter for hunters*), huddled together during rifle season. We sat on chairs in the blind from before sunrise to nearly dusk in below freezing temperatures, waiting for a buck to possibly come out and feed on clover in the open field. I told him to be patient. You can't shoot a deer if you're not out here in the woods. Lunches were packed in the morning, and we were in this for the long haul. Tucker was one of the most patient young men I have ever known, sitting there all day with never a complaint. Finally, just before dusk, an eight-pointer came out. Tucker aimed and shot, certain he had hit the buck. The buck took off running, so we stepped out of the blind and walked back to Grandpa's house to warm up and waited a bit before returning to the woods to track it. Dad, Grandpa, Tucker, Tanner, and I went to look for it. Checking the spot where it was standing when shot, we saw no visible blood, which is not a sure sign of a good shot. No blood was found nearby. The area was combed more thoroughly, but there were still no signs of blood, so it was decided to wait until the next morning to go back out out and search. Tucker was sure he had made a good shot and was so excited he didn't sleep. Neither did I. I so wanted him to have that buck. Sunrise finally arrived, and we all got dressed and went out to track the buck in the morning light. It took a while, but we found it. Tucker's first eight-pointer—with Mom. How cool was that! Photos were taken of Tucker and I with the deer. I mounted the horns for him, which are proudly displayed in his bedroom. Tucker really enjoyed hunting and spent a lot of hours in the woods. Because of his age, I was with him and enjoyed that hunting time together. On one other hunting venture we were on, he would not admit his fingers were cold and nearly froze the tips of his fingers off because he did not bring gloves with him. I gave up a pair of my gloves so he could stay longer, just waiting for a chance to shoot a deer with his bow. We ended up seeing nothing that night, but he was bound and determined not to leave early just in case a buck showed.

About Tucker

Tucker was very protective of his belongings and his "all boy" room. When he was growing up, he wanted a door sign posted that said, "No girls allowed." No girls except Mom, that is. Special sentimental items cherished by him adorned his room like his deer horns, Grandpa's bear rug, an autographed Packer football, and an autographed Athens baseball. His favorite TV show was *Impractical Jokers*. If you haven't seen this comedy show, four friends think up funny pranks that they dare each other to do. Failure to follow through means consequences. Tucker watched and rewatched the shows, fed off their funny characters, loved a good prank, and enjoyed having fun. I had always wondered how he would think up a quick-wit response or a comic comeback so quickly. This show sure taught him well. Both comedies and Old Westerns were enjoyed by Tucker. Clint Eastwood's and John Wayne's decoupaged Old Western photos hung on each side of the deer shoulder mount in his room. These types of shows also took after Dad's interests as well.

Tucker had a fascination and love for all types of animals. So often on those early vacation trips, Tucker had to have a photo taken, or took his own photo, of every animal, real or statue, that he came across. I made up his own private photo albums. He had a special love for bald eagles. When the four-day fair came to Athens every August, Tanner and Tucker would spend their money at the cap gun shooting game. They would each shoot until they had enough winning coupons to get a pretty nice prize by the last day of the fair on Sunday. Tucker usually came home with bald eagle statues. Each one was a little different than the next. So many were won over the years that he had a bald eagle collection, which I kept on display in a curio cabinet in our living room. He had asked me to save them so they could be placed in his house when he got married.

Tucker always expressed interest in wanting a family and kids. I shared with him stories of our courtship years, which lasted throughout high school and continued on after high school until Dad finally broke down and asked me to get married after seventeen years. He liked to hear about our relationship and placed a two-picture frame on a shelf in his room. On one side of the frame was a copy of our newspaper wedding photo announcement and on the other was a grade school photo of Dad. His wish was to have a wife, lots of kids, and family like we had. I often thought he would be a great dad and looked forward to that time when he'd marry and have a bunch of little ones as he always put family first. In middle school, the class was given an assignment to write down the top thirty things one wanted to do before he or she died. Number 1 on his list—get married. Tucker and I joked that I wanted him to have a football team of grandkids and that I'd help take care of them. He told me, "I can do that, Mom!" He knew I had wanted more children in the home. Family was very important to Tucker, and it meant everything to me.

Family pets

Our first family pet was a black Pomeranian named Shimmy. Tucker took her loss hard when we had to put her down due to old age. At age twelve, I told Tucker he could get a dog. His choice was another Pomeranian. After a bit of a search, a purebred black male with brown highlights was found for sale. I had a dream the night we brought that Pom home that we should call him Shadow. When I told Tucker about my dream, the name stuck. Tucker loved his dog, brushing his hair and teeth, playing with him, taking him for walks, and giving him treats.

Relationships with others

Friends meant the world to Tucker, and he was just about as protective of them as he was with his room, thinking highly of them and enjoying hanging out with them. Tucker exhibited a special, rare quality in his relationships with others. He may not have always understood others but seemed to see the good in a person instead of speaking poorly of them. I think that is part of why he was loved by so many. Not only by the way he conducted himself with others but by making himself available when help was needed. He was dependable, and one could count on him. I witnessed these traits in how he related to all different types of people.

That is why writing this book hurts. Much needs to be shared about him and how he has touched so many. Good that has come out of such a sad situation. His story and events that happened after his death will give others something to think about that although he is not here in physical being, he is still giving in a spiritual way. In his death, this world has missed out on what this young man had to offer so many here on earth.

Sentiments from Mom

Sometimes you cannot put into words the connection shared with another. I had this special connection with Tucker. It was just there. He understood me, and I understood him. The conversations shared while we sat on his bed many a time will not be forgotten. I sensed when something was bothering him, and he was willing to open up and talk about it. He cried when his feelings were hurt and felt comfortable sharing with me what happened to cause his sadness. From a very young age, every night before bed, we hugged and said together, "Now I Lay Me Down to Sleep." After that I got a big hug, kiss, and an "I love you, Mom" before he turned and tucked his head into the pillow each night. I recall all that started to change at about age eleven, when he started to think he was a big boy. Then it was just a pleasant "Good night, Mom."

My job as a multiline insurance claims representative allows me to work out of my home. Most mornings I was at work before Tucker got up. My office is next to his bedroom. When he got up, I would say "Morning, Tuck." He would say "Morning, Mom" right back. It wasn't anything special, but it was the way we said it that made it special. It was "our way." Before every meal, Tucker made a point of starting the prayer "Come, Lord Jesus, be our guest. Let this food to us be blessed." Tucker believed in prayer, in Jesus, in the Bible, and religion.

The special ring

I like to wear jewelry and wanted a special ring to signify my two boys so I could wear it all the time. The ring was designed containing two small square emeralds reflective of the boys' May birthstones with diamonds and baguettes mounted down each side. A local jeweler put my idea into a uniquely styled ring, which I still wear today. After wearing it a few years, I lost one of the emeralds. I was crushed. The ring is one of a kind, and each stone is precious to me because of the meaning behind it. Little did I know just how precious the stone is until I lost it and just how significant, and similar, the loss would mirror what was going to happen in the future. I did replace the stone with a larger pear-shaped emerald stone. But in my heart, the ring would never be the same. How true those same words would be spoken not too far in the future. Tucker was not replaceable.

Let the story begin

I am so glad Tucker and I shared what time we had together. With all my love and a terribly broken heart, now you have a little background about Tucker. What follows next is my story in honor of my son and his short stay with us on earth.

HERE FOR A GOOD TIME, NOT A LONG TIME

Baby Photos

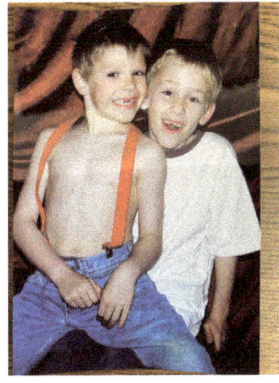

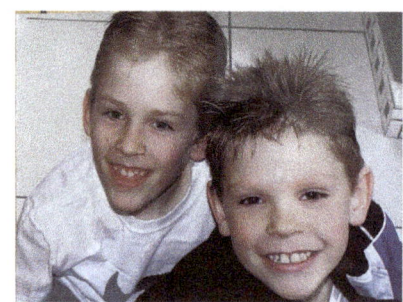

Tanner & Tucker
The Brothers

HERE FOR A GOOD TIME, NOT A LONG TIME

Mom & The Boys

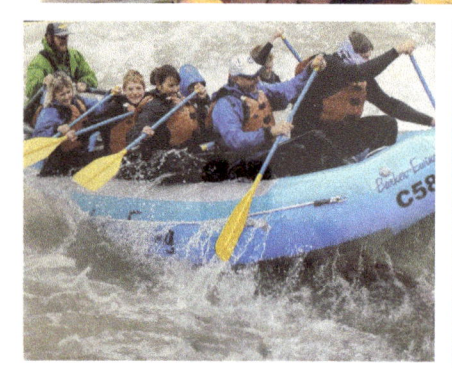

Vacation Times

HERE FOR A GOOD TIME, NOT A LONG TIME

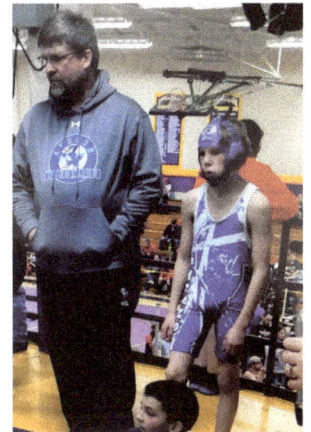

Coach Dad

Good Times With Friends Doing Community Service Work At The Cemetery

HERE FOR A GOOD TIME, NOT A LONG TIME

Three Sport Athlete

23

TRACY WESTFALL

Married June 6, 1998

Godparents Aunt Lorene
& Corey Westfall

Eagle Collection

CHAPTER 2

Weeks Leading Up to the Accident

Reflecting back, I can't help but think I recognized early signs that Tucker would not be with us on earth very long.

I had questioned why. Why did I watch him so closely? Why did I want to hang out with him? Why did I want him near me? I would look at Tucker like it would be the last time I would see him. Little did I know…or did I know? Why did I feel this way? I would try to memorize everything about him—his smell, his skin, his nose, his laugh, and his character. I loved running my fingers through a fresh buzz haircut or giving him a big ole hug. Tucker would join me on the couch on Wednesday nights to watch our favorite show, *SEAL Team*. Wednesday was also the evening when we had one of the few "family sit-down" mealtimes all together. We could all talk. I so enjoyed the family conversations, Dad teasing the boys about girls, and the boys sharing what happened at school or after school. Wednesday night was when Dad had no evening school obligations, no late practices, no games, no matches, and no meetings. Wednesday nights were family night.

The following is a summary of happenings that lead up to his accident, which makes one question if Tucker may have been aware his days were numbered. This series of events has kept me wondering that all of this was supposed to have taken place. As if it had for a reason.

Junior Prom, April 2018

As I mentioned earlier, Tucker truly enjoyed being with his friends. Tucker and his buddies, girls and guys, made plans to attend the 2018 Junior Prom their freshman year. He didn't give me much notice that he was planning on going to the prom, asking me just a day before if I had suspenders, a bow tie, and a nice shirt for him to wear. Scrambling to pull together a nice outfit for him, I remember telling him to give me a little more notice next time! Moments later, he was swiping his iPhone and showed me a swatch of the color of Shauna Belter's dress that she was wearing and asked if I had anything around the house to match. I did not know he had a date for prom and went on to ask him further about Shauna. He said he didn't have a date, that Shauna and he were going just as "friends." Well, okay, and I smiled at him…whatever.

So I'm going through closets and drawers looking for the items needed to outfit him. Where are those maroon-colored suspenders that Dad wore in high school? Fortunately, I found them in a drawer and was so glad Dad had kept them all these years! My mom had given me a number of bow ties in black and red that Dad and Grandpa had worn years ago, along with some cuff links. I found those in the back of a bedroom dresser drawer and pulled out one of the black bow ties and a set of cuff links. Then I ran upstairs and pulled Tucker's white church shirt with black buttons off a hanger from a closet and brought out a nice pair of black dress slacks. I gathered up everything and took it to Tucker to have him try on everything to see how it fit. Boy, he was decked out looking so handsome and ready for some photos. One last item to accent his outfit was my grandpa's gray felt hat with a feather. Mom told me Grandpa wore this particular hat to Sunday church often. The hat was given to me as a keepsake after Grandpa died, and it finished Tucker's outfit perfectly. Now he was wearing a little of the past from both sides of my family.

Looking dashing and debonair, Tucker was always open to posing for photos. Those looks and poses he had practiced using his cell phone now came in handy, some serious, others with a smile. He liked acting like he was a model and could change his expression on a dime. Little did I know that only weeks later, I would be pulling these special pictures to select one for his obituary. Tucker dressed in his outfit the following day, attended the pre-prom activities, and had prom photos taken with his friends that evening. These photos are some of my most cherished photos and remain displayed specially framed on my living room entertainment center. Just by looking at the photos, it is apparent that his friends meant so much to him. I have come to learn what a truly great group of friends he had and how lucky he was to have had these special times together with them.

A few weeks before the accident

It was a few weeks before the accident that I had a dream where Tucker was driving a tractor and turned short into a field driveway. The tractor rolled over. I woke up crying, not wanting Tucker to enroll in the Tractor Safety Course being offered to allow him to drive tractors at Miltrim Farms for Uncle Tom. After the accident, I wondered if the tractor was actually the UTV, and I was seeing the future accident.

Discussion about God

Later, after the accident, Dale shared a story with me that he had overheard Tucker and his friends at school discussing God one day. It seemed like an unusual conversation for kids to be having. Dad later asked Tucker if he believed in God, and he replied, "Yes. Tanner is the person you need to worry about."

Discussion about future proms

It was one of those conversations when I was sitting with Tucker on his bed, going over the school annual photos. We got on the subject about prom and how his junior class prom was coming up in a couple of years, so I had asked if he was interested in being on prom court. He made a comment back to me saying something like "what happens if I don't make it." My initial thoughts were that this was a strange response, but I responded that it wouldn't matter. I would still want to be there to help decorate and watch as it was such a special night, and I enjoyed seeing everyone dressed up. He just looked down and kept turning the pages of the annual. Again, I thought to myself that this was odd. Now, looking back, I cannot help but wonder if he knew he wasn't going to be around for his junior prom.

A week or so before the accident

Our family attended several of the May 2018 graduation parties. This was not unusual since Dad is a coach and teacher, so our family was usually invited to a number of parties. At one graduation party, our family was sitting around the table, chatting with a couple whose son-in-law deals in sports cars. I asked them if they had any contacts in getting a nice used sports car for Tucker because driver's education training was to begin after the school year was finished in a couple of weeks. Tucker did not make eye contact with me and seemed disinterested, simply responding like, "Okay, Mom." It was somewhat of a letdown for me. I expected an excited reaction, knowing I was even suggesting a sports car, but he hadn't reacted with the enthusiasm of a young man getting his first car. Again, I can't help but wonder if he had sensed he wouldn't be here. It was just another sign I had reflected back on.

Hunting vacation

One last memory that stands out that maybe Tucker didn't know he'd be here is when Tucker was sitting in the kitchen chair he "claimed" as his spot. We were discussing going on a family Alaskan hunting vacation after he graduated in May 2021 because Dad was planning to retire after Tucker graduated and would be able to hunt for an extended period. I brought up possible ways to travel there, where we could stay, how long we could stay, and what we could hunt and fish. Tucker kept his head down and did not make eye contact with me and didn't say much. I thought it strange at the time, but now again, reflecting back, maybe he knew he wasn't going to be around to share this ultimate vacation with us. After losing Tucker, that Alaskan vacation has kind of lost its luster. The family doesn't have a desire to go anywhere knowing one of the family will always be missing.

May 30, 2018, three days before the accident

The 2018 Athens Fighting Bluejays High School baseball team had a mix of some very good athletes. Their regular baseball season ended with a 20–2 record, being ranked number one in the division, earning the right to proceed to post-season tournament play.

Regionals was held at the Athens High School baseball field. Tucker was a high school freshman and did not get to play in the game but was a future player and very proud to be in the dugout as part of the team. Between innings, he was one of the players who ran down the third baseline to the outfield fence and turned back around, running back to the dugout. This was a customary practice for the nonstarters to stretch out between innings.

The final regional game against Northland Lutheran, ranked number two, would determine what team was headed to sectionals. The weather was cold and miserable. There was a forty-five-minute rain delay. The infield was full of puddles. Athens ended up winning that game 10–0 and was headed to sectionals to be held on June 5. Excitement for the baseball team was growing in the Athens community with the possibility of getting to the state tournament. A team photo with the regionals plaque was taken on that rainy day. This would be Tucker's last photo.

May 31, 2018

Our elderly neighbor, Eugene Denk, dropped by, had a seat on our front porch, joined us for a cold beer and a pleasant visit. Tucker came out to say hi and told Mr. Denk how he was going to be picking rocks that upcoming Saturday for his Uncle Tom at Miltrim Farms. Tucker was just that kind of guy going out of his way to come outside and engage in a conversation. He enjoyed the young and old.

June 1, 2018, the firepit

    The night of June 1, 2018, Tucker had two friends over for supper. I had just finished constructing a firepit that Tucker wanted in the backyard as many in the neighborhood were having firepit parties, and he had asked me for one so he could have friends gather at our house too. Dale, I, and the three boys broke it in that early June evening. Tucker and his friends lifted a picnic table that was up near the house and walked it down to the firepit. With the fire started, I brought down paper plates, condiments, and stakes to roast wieners in celebration of the new firepit. The boys ate. We chatted a bit, enjoying the fire and each other's company, then the guys left, walking over to a neighbor's house for a firepit party happening there for the remainder of the evening. Tucker and one of the two friends who had been at supper earlier needed to be home by 11:00 p.m., knowing they needed to get up for work in the morning at Miltrim Farms to pick rocks. Picking rocks on a farmer's field is when there is a need to have the larger rocks picked out by hand so that when the crops are harvested, the hay bins and other farm equipment that travel on the fields do not get damaged by large rocks. The rocks have to be picked by hand and are placed on a wagon, a truck, or in the back of a UTV to be hauled away from the field. Tucker was proud he had organized his first crew to pick rocks.

    A (girl) friend of Tucker's (also a classmate of Tanner) later told me that she was the one who dropped Tucker off at the house that last night. He had stepped out of her vehicle, and she said, "Love you!" Tuck responded back, "Love you too!" Tucker ended up sleeping in Tanner's bed that night because his friend slept in Tucker's bed. Tanner was not home for the evening, as he and Grandma Westfall had left earlier that day to travel down to La Crosse, Wisconsin, to watch the Wisconsin State track finals competition.

HERE FOR A GOOD TIME, NOT A LONG TIME

Pre-Prom Fun
April 2018

TRACY WESTFALL

Prom
April 2018

HERE FOR A GOOD TIME, NOT A LONG TIME

Regional Champs
Last Photo Taken Of Tucker (#12)

CHAPTER 3

The Accident—Saturday, June 2, 2018

It was just a regular Saturday morning with everyone getting ready to go their separate ways with activities planned for the day. It was a bit cloudy and still cool for an early Central Wisconsin summer day in June.

About 7:00 a.m., just an hour and a half before Tucker's accident, Dad had already been busy loading his four-wheeler ATV onto his truck. He then said his goodbye to me and headed out for a four-wheeler bachelor party being held up in northern Wisconsin for a friend who would be marrying soon.

At 8:00 a.m., I cooked scrambled eggs for Tucker and his friend who stayed overnight. After eating their eggs and drinking a glass of chocolate milk, Tucker filled a blue tote cooler with a couple of Ice Mountain plastic bottles of water. He was wearing his brown Driftless Angler logo cap, a pair of blue jeans, and a wrestling T-shirt. They were asked to report to Uncle Tom at Miltrim Farms at 8:30 a.m. for instructions on where they would be picking rocks for the day, so Tucker tied up his steel-toed boots, then both boys left the house and jumped into my car for a ride to the farm. Tucker was in the front passenger seat next to me, and his friend sat behind Tucker in the back seat.

At 8:28 a.m., I started to back out of our driveway just as an older couple drove up and stopped to ask where the cemetery was. I offered to have them follow me so I could lead them to the cemetery since it was located near our home. When we arrived, they waved a thank you as they passed by to enter into one of the cemetery driveways.

I turned my car around and headed to pick up Tucker's other friend/classmate. After his friend jumped in, I drove out to Miltrim Farms, which was located just over two miles directly west of our house, outside of the Village of Athens. The route also went directly past Athens High School and the sports fields. It took just under five minutes to make the trip.

Miltrim Farms is a large operation consisting of several large milking barns, equipment storage buildings, and the main office building. At the time, there was a new robot milking barn and visitor center under construction on the property as well. Uncle Tom was waiting out in front of the workshop and milk house area as we drove in. There was a UTV ready for the boys to use to load the rocks into.

At 8:33 a.m., Tucker and his friends got out of my car and greeted Uncle Tom. I was still sitting in my car with my window down, overhearing Uncle Tom instructing the boys to scan the field for the rocks since two haybines had been recently damaged due to hitting larger rocks on the particular field they were headed to. I watched the boys get into the UTV. Tucker was in the driver's seat, one friend was seated in the middle, and the other got in on the right side. Tucker had picked rocks in the past couple of years and had driven this UTV before working under the direction of Tanner. I recall being so proud and pleased to see signs of Tucker growing up and taking charge by arranging his own crew for this morning's work. They were ready to pull out with the UTV, so I drove away and headed back for home.

I did not know the exact events that occurred once I left the driveway but later learned that they were going south about a mile and a quarter down Silver Leaf Road to a field to pick the rocks. Due to the vast amount of acreage Miltrim Farms owns, the only way to access many of the properties is to take the secondary roads, as you are not allowed to cross over other people's properties.

Then it happened. The day. The time. Forever etched in memory.

Four-tenths of a mile down Silver Leaf Road was as far as the boys traveled before the accident occurred. They had made it just past the Miltrim Farms property boundary line and were in front of the adjoining Amish farm located next door on the same west side of the road as Miltrim Farms. The mailbox owned by the Amish family was located just off the gravel road, mounted on a metal post into a steel wheel, which rested on the ground, holding it in place on the north side of their driveway entrance.

Tucker lost control of the UTV. The UTV veered suddenly to the right and started to head toward the grass ditch. Tucker corrected to get back onto the gravel road. The UTV struck the sturdy mailbox post. The right front wheel and axle area caught the solid post. It caused the UTV to make a sudden stop and go into a forward flip. The UTV landed on all four wheels in the west ditch just south of the Amish driveway's culvert.

There were no side doors or catch fencing on the UTV to keep them in the UTV. The boys were not seat belted, nor were they wearing helmets.

The friend seated on the right side of the UTV was ejected from the passenger side of the UTV. He recalls flying through the air and landing in the grass on the west side ditch, beyond where the UTV ended up. The friend sitting in the middle was thrust forward. The impact caused the UTV windshield to pop out. He flew through the windshield opening. He landed near the west edge of the gravel road where the grass in the ditch starts.

It has not ever been totally made clear to me on how Tucker was ejected.

I learned of these details later from Tucker's friend and the Amish farmer who tried to render CPR to Tucker. It is my opinion that when the UTV struck the mailbox, Tucker's head may have hit the upper right corner or pillar of the UTV. The rooftop of the UTV was cracked. He had a dislocated right shoulder so that had made impact with something hard. Once thrown from the UTV, his body had skidded across the driveway, landing on the high grass and coming to rest in the ditch. Later, I confirmed the 911 call was dispatched at 8:38 a.m.

So back to the moments before I learned of the accident. I did return home from dropping the boys off, and the volunteer EMT who lives near our house was backing his vehicle out of his driveway as I passed by. He had to place his vehicle back into drive and pull back into his driveway to allow me to pass. Had I only known at that moment that he was responding to Tucker…Tucker was the emergency! I drove into my driveway, placed the vehicle in park, ran into the house to pick up a few items to go run errands. It was the first day of my vacation, so I was planning to head to Marshfield, a nearby city, to do some shopping.

At 8:53 a.m., I got back into my car to leave, and the cell phone was ringing as I had left the phone in my vehicle. I saw it was Uncle Tom calling. I thought right away that I had heard sirens going off and was thinking this was not good wherever they were headed. I picked up the call. Uncle Tom informed me of the accident and said to come back to the farm as CPR was being done on Tucker. Thinking, *oh no*, and *please be all right*, I drove back to the farm and arrived on scene by 8:57 a.m.

I saw the UTV sitting on all four wheels, facing west in the ditch on Silver Leaf Road, which runs in a north to south direction. The ambulance was on site; the fire department was in the open field on the east side of Silver Leaf, setting up for Flight for Life. Lights were flashing, and county sheriff's officers were on site. I drove up as close as I could get and parked my vehicle on the road. As I was getting out of the vehicle and approaching the officers, they stopped me and inquired who I was. I told them I was Tucker's mom. They directed me to move my vehicle from the east side of the road to the south side of the road past the Amish driveway. So I got back into my vehicle and moved it as requested. When I got back out, I reapproached the officers. The first officer asked me if Tucker was involved in horseplay. I told him I was not there, so his friends would be the persons to ask. I could see by the look on the second officer's face that this situation was not good. The officers asked me a few more questions about my name, where my husband was, and some other questions. The ambulance had moved from the Amish owner's driveway to the east side of Silver Leaf facing north. I asked EMT personnel outside of the ambulance if I could see Tucker. An EMT responded that they were working on Tucker.

Uncle Tom and Aunt Lorene were walking around the scene of the accident. I told Tom not to walk on the driveway or kick the dirt. My job is an insurance adjuster. I deal with fatalities, severe accidents, and other types of commercial, homeowner, and auto losses as a part of my daily job. Part of this job entails securing a scene as I understand the importance of protecting a scene and securing evidence. I remember the officers questioning me about how calm I was and me explaining to them what I did for a living and how I have been exposed to tragic events where I need to maintain my composure to collect facts.

I noticed Tucker's friends were sitting on the grass in front of the Amish family's home. The brother and sister of one of the friends had already arrived on scene, and they were assisting their brother to their truck so they could take him to a medical facility to have him checked out. Before they left, I ran over to the truck and asked him who had called 911. He explained to me that he had made the initial call but had given his phone to the Amish man to talk to the dispatcher. The dispatcher was instructing him on how to perform CPR over the phone. I then asked him how he was and received a quick response that he wanted to get his knee and leg checked out. A quick glance back to the Amish driveway and I see the other friend's dad escorting him to their truck. I still was unable to see Tucker but knew I had to get in touch with Dale right away.

At 9:04 a.m., I attempted to call Dale, but he did not pick up on his cell phone, so I left a voice message that this was about Tucker and to call because it was an emergency.

At 9:14 a.m., there was still no word from Dale yet, so I called Grandpa Westfall so he could have someone to get in touch with Dale. Grandpa's voice was shaken when I told him Tucker was in an accident, and I needed get in touch with Dale as soon as possible. I then texted Tanner (if you recall, he was with Grandma Westfall in La Crosse at the state track finals). With cell phones these days, the word spread quickly, and he already knew about the accident. He wanted to know where to go. I instructed him to just come home.

I remained at the scene, taking photos as if I was conducting any other investigation. Right away, I assessed that the tire tracks were going straight, then made an abrupt right turn toward the ditch. Why? I saw the windshield in the middle of the driveway but recalled being told earlier that the windshield had been moved by a passerby because it was lying in the roadway. The Amish owner's mailbox had been tossed from the metal pole and steel wheel where it had previously been attached. The pole was bent. Walking over to the west ditch, I saw blood on the grass just past the driveway culvert. This had to be where the EMTs found Tucker. His cap he had on and the blue cooler he had put the plastic water bottles in just a little over a half hour earlier were in the driveway. I then went over and photographed the UTV still positioned in the west ditch.

At 9:52 a.m., Dale tried to call me (*he told me this later*), but we couldn't connect. He left where he was to get to better cell reception. In his haste, he forgot to strap down the four-wheeler, and it fell off the back of his truck, rolling into the roadway. He stopped and had to take the time to get it back on the truck and then proceeded to get to a place where he had cell service to call me.

Meanwhile, the ambulance personnel allowed me inside their unit. This may not have been customary practice; however, we are a small community where everyone knows everyone, so they did appear to make an exception. I stepped into the ambulance. Tucker was lying on the gurney. His eyes were closed. They had taken off his shirt and pants to check for injuries, so he was just in his underwear. I saw his boots perfectly aligned next to his feet on the floor of the ambulance. There were a number of EMT personnel inside, but my focus was on Tucker. An EMT had on gloves and was holding white thick bandages on the right side of Tucker's head behind his ear. I glanced over Tucker's body. There did not appear to be any severe injuries, cuts, or fractures. I made a mental note that he was wearing brown underwear (keep this color in mind when you read the autopsy chapter coming up). I was glad to see he was wearing good underwear with no holes in them. The EMT showed me the heart rate machine where there was no heartbeat. An EMT opened Tucker's eyes for me, but there was no response to light. I asked them to remove the bandage behind the ear. They did not want to. I asked them again, and the EMT did for a brief moment. When the EMT removed the gauze, blood came out. It was at that moment I knew Tucker was no longer with us. I told them to stop pumping to try to revive him as it was of no use. Tucker's body was lifeless. He was gone, having died instantly, suffering a skull injury. His spirit had already left his body. It was then that I vaguely heard the EMT say they could not stop pumping his chest because they were providing a service and needed to continue. I took one last look at Tucker, looked up with tearful eyes, and thanked them. I stepped out of the ambulance.

Lorene met me outside of the ambulance and asked how he was. I said, "It is a fatality." She cupped her hands in her face and hunched over, grabbing her knees. She came up and hugged me. I hugged her back. She left, and I went back to the scene. An EMT had handed me Tucker's phone at some point while I was outside the ambulance. I later learned Flight for Life was unable to take off due to the cloud cover that morning, so they would not be responding to the scene. It would not have made a difference in Tucker's case. He had died upon impact.

At 10:07 a.m., Dale finally got through on his cell. He wanted to know what happened. I told him Tucker was in an accident. He jokingly said, "Well, is he alive?" I responded flatly, "No, please come home." There was silence. I knew he felt what I felt—like the world had just come crashing down around us. This couldn't be real. We couldn't be living this. This was not happening. No further conversation was exchanged until he returned home.

Understandably, my memory of the next moments and hours was not that clear. I was in disbelief. There wasn't anything I could do. There wasn't anything anyone could do. Shock and numbness were starting to take over.

Lorene had returned to the accident scene and was with me. The ambulance left the scene to take Tucker to the coroner to pronounce him dead. The officers indicated they were having the Department of Natural Resources (DNR) and a reconstructionist come out to the scene. Wisconsin law requires a DNR report to be filed within ten days of the incident when an ATV or UTV is involved.

We stayed at the scene a bit longer and realized there was nothing else we could do. The ambulance had left. The fire department had removed the safety cones from the field that were meant for Flight for Life and left. What came to mind now was that our parents needed to be told, but not by phone. This needed to be handled face-to-face. Lorene and I drove our separate vehicles to our parents' home located about three miles away from where the accident occurred. Our dad had just left the house to go mow lawn at one of the farms that Miltrim Farms owns. Dad is in his early eighties and helps with running errands and keeping the lawns trimmed. Lorene contacted Tom who went to find Dad *(Tucker's grandfather)* to tell him what happened. It was apparent to our parents that something had happened as the sheriff's patrol car with the sirens blaring raced right past their home to get to the accident.

Lorene and I drove into our parents' driveway and got out of our vehicles. Mom stuck her head out of the doorway of the house to greet us when we arrived and came outside. Mom was always glad to see us. We approached her on the walkway leading to our childhood home. Her look, her emotions quickly changed as I could barely get the words out. "Tucker was in an accident, and he is no longer with us." Mom wasn't sure she heard correctly. Lorene then tried to get the words out. Mom couldn't believe it and didn't know what to say. I heard her whisper, "I have never gone through this before." We all stood outside for a moment, then Mom told us to come inside.

We went into the house, and I explained to Mom again, in general, what had happened. We stood in the kitchen, where we had so many family gatherings while growing up. This was not a gathering we could have ever imagined having.

Lorene used her cell phone to call our sister, Wanda, to relay to her what had just happened. She handed the phone to Mom to do the talking, unable herself to get the words out. Wanda had just returned to Colorado, where she resides, just two days earlier. She had been visiting in Athens to attend the funeral services of another person our family was close to who had passed away just the Saturday before. He was a neighbor and like a second father to us.

My brother, Steve, and his wife, Jessica, and their son, Marcus, arrived at the house. They had been at the annual Athens Future Farmers of America (FFA) pancake breakfast event going on that morning. I saw Jessica text her family in Peru to notify them. Everyone just stood around in the kitchen. Kind of a numb, no one knew what to do, what to say. The news was shocking. It was just starting to sink in.

Dale had texted me that he was home. I said my goodbyes and left my family, driving the three miles back to Athens to meet Dale at our home. When I entered the house, Dale was sitting on the couch in the living room. I sat down next to him and shared what information I could about what happened. When I finished, we hugged and cried. Grandpa Westfall showed up shortly thereafter and was told what happened. We waited for Tanner and Grandma Westfall to return from La Crosse. They arrived about a half hour later. I met them at the front door. I told them Tucker did not make it and fell into Tanner's arms and hugged him. Grandma Westfall burst into tears and joined her husband and son in the living room.

The mom of one of the friends who were in the UTV with Tucker called and inquired which hospital Tucker was taken to so her son could go visit him. I told her Tucker didn't make it. There was silence at first and then an "Oh my god" or something. I was not able to speak any longer and disconnected the call.

I went into the kitchen and started to make spaghetti and meat sauce as this was one of Tucker's favorite meals. He and his friend were supposed to have that for lunch once they returned from picking rocks. Subconsciously, I guess I wanted this not to be true and wanted things to go on as planned. The coroner phoned on our landline a short time later. I took the call as no one else could speak. How was I able to? Another strong moment, trying to keep the family in check, I guess. The coroner asked some questions and formally pronounced his death, indicating Tucker's body would be taken for an autopsy.

Word had spread quickly throughout our small village. Most people knew each other or each other's family. They certainly knew our family given Dale's involvement as a teacher, coach, and former local high school athlete.

Relatives started to drop by the house. Friends brought food, gifts, and extended their sympathies. Condolences went on throughout the remainder of that day and the days that followed. Our home was like a revolving door. Many of Dale's former Athens High School athletes and students showed up with a whole lot of tears and hugs exchanged.

That evening, I went up to Tucker's room and walked in. A rush *(or I describe it as a flush)* came over me. I can't explain it. It was like I walked into a wall of lovingness that went into me—through me. I talked to Tucker right then and there—the same place where we had talked so many times before while sitting on his bed. I told him I knew he was in his room. This was his retreat, his sanctuary. Whatever this rush was, it was a remarkable feeling of all goodness and love. I can't explain it any other way. After sitting on the bed for a bit, I left his room, walked down a short hallway leading to my office, sat down on the computer, and prepared Tucker's obituary. It took just a short time to write it since all the words just seemed to flow easily.

The following day, friends and so many in the community continued to visit. There were numerous gatherings in our living room. A relative who is on Facebook and Instagram often asked me if I had any idea what Tucker had used to set up his Instagram account. Of course, I did not and had no experience in using this computer app. She went on to share that his Instagram motto read, "Here for a good time, not a long time." How meaningful is that? Why would Tucker have used that? Did he know something? Many of those earlier signs I mentioned came to mind.

Tucker had looked up to many athletes in school. Austin Engel was one of them. He had great wrestling skills, and Tucker wanted to be like him. His sister had designed a special symbolic logo of a set of angel wings with a halo over a *T*. On each side of the letter *T* was the number 1 and the number 2. The number 12 was Tucker's baseball uniform number. This logo has come to represent him. Later, the same logo design was made with Tucker's football number—number 22. Car stickers were made of both, and many people in the village had Tucker's symbols displayed on their vehicles within days of the accident.

Later that afternoon, we met with the funeral director in town and decided there would be no visitation, only the funeral, and the funeral would be held at the high school.

On June 4, 2018, the Engel family, including Austin, came over. They had made one-of-a-kind Athens Bluejay T-shirts for our family with a heart and the number 12 inside of it. Dad and mine had the word *son* imprinted in blue sparkling letters on the side of the sleeve. Tanner's had the word *brother* on the sleeve with those same sparkling letters.

The baseball team and coaches walked to our home, bringing with them their heavy hearts with their heads bowed down. I was told later they had walked side by side, two in a row, down the street, to our door. There was a knock on the door, and one by one, they entered our home. Every coach's and player's face was full of tears as they gave warm hugs to Dale, me, and Tanner. I asked Coach Bill Coker if they could all have a seat in our living room. He questioned me on that and asked if I really wanted to speak with the team. I responded promptly that I wanted to because I thought it was important.

I knew by now that most of them had heard details of the accident, so I wanted to make sure I told them that we didn't have all the facts but that Tucker lost control of the UTV and tried to correct the UTV striking a mailbox. This caused the sudden stop and a front rollover. Tucker hit his head and died instantly. All the details still needed to be investigated, but we know he did not suffer. I encouraged the team to be strong and focus on winning the sectionals tournament scheduled for the day before Tucker's funeral. The team earned the right to be there, and I knew it would be very important to Tucker to go on winning without him. I told them to go out and score twenty-five runs. Dale needed to do his part and coach just like this was any other game. He was leaning up against the French doors of our bedroom looking into the living room at the team and meekly replied, "I will try." It was a very emotional "coming together" moment. I think those kids needed to hear this and drew strength, determination, and unity that day. They left knowing they needed to really come together as a team, fight for the next game, and carry on as that state championship was in their sights. Not only to win this for themselves but win for Tucker! This tragedy could only make them stronger, having more incentive than ever to make this happen. Tucker's sudden death and what lay ahead over the next week had now set this team on an emotionally charged mission. Achieving a repeat of that state championship held special meaning now more than ever.

After the team and coaches left our home, a short time later, the pastor arrived. He was given personal information about Tucker so that he could prepare for the funeral.

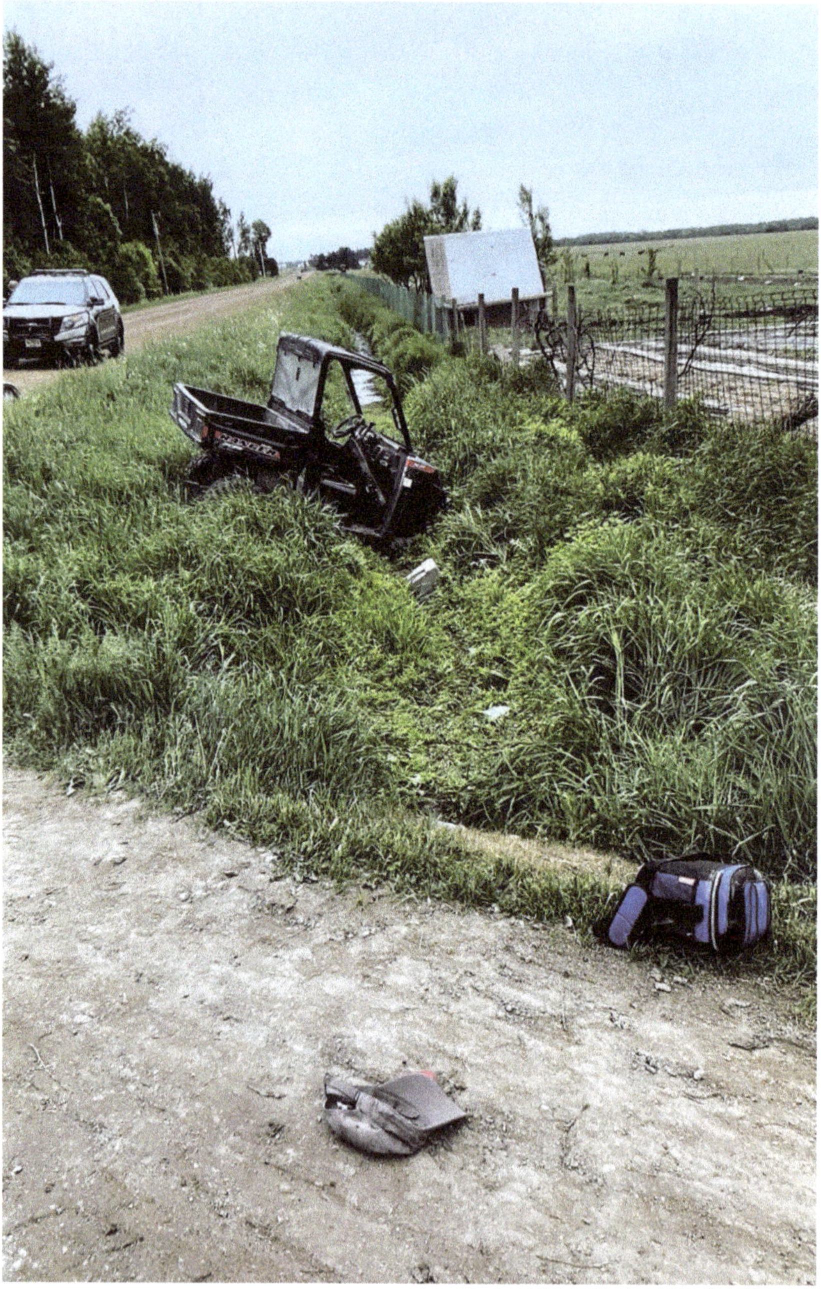

CHAPTER 4

Athens High School Baseball Sectionals—Tuesday, June 5, 2018

The Athens Fighting Bluejays baseball team headed to the WIAA Division 4 Sectionals tournament on Tuesday, June 5, 2018, in White Lake, Wisconsin, under sunny, clear blue skies. White Lake is an even smaller rural town than Athens with a population less than 350. The town is only an hour and a half drive from Athens. It was a great turnout by the Athens faithful who were there to support the team. Those who made the road trip brought their lawn chairs and strategically placed them down the first baseline outside the metal fences of the groomed and neatly lined baseball field.

The team came out with Tucker's T12 logo on the back of their ball caps and the logo was being sported on the left sleeve of their jerseys. How could they have been done so quickly? All I could think was that some seamstress must have been up all night to get this done in time for the game, as the accident had happened only a couple days ago. A yellow monarch butterfly flew around the field most of the day. A relative commented that it was Tucker. He knew where we were and wouldn't miss it, knowing the important significance of this day. We felt his presence.

Two tournament games were played that day. Tucker's white number 12 baseball jersey was hung in the dugout. Tanner had also joined the team in the dugout. Announcers from WKEB99.3 FM,

Medford radio, were seated in front of the Athens fans and provided radio commentary for both games. Many Athens area people who could not attend due to their work schedules tuned in on their radios to listen to the game being broadcasted.

The semifinal game was against Pittsville. The final score ended up 14–1 with Athens taking the win in five innings. In high school baseball, if there is a ten-run lead after five innings, the game concludes versus the teams playing the full seven innings. This win meant Athens advanced to the final game of the day, the sectional championship game against Wausaukee. Athens won in five innings with a no-hitter and final score of 10–0.

As the game ended, someone encouraged me to go to the dugout where my husband, Assistant Coach Dale, was standing. I recall thinking, *No I can't do that. This is a forbidden area for anyone but the team and coaches.* But I found myself walking from the place I was standing on the fence line onto the grass leading to the dugout and heading into the dugout where Dale was standing. It was just a spontaneous reaction on my part that I jumped up and gave him a big hug, cradling my legs around him. When I jumped back down to the ground, he looked me in the eyes and asked me if I wanted to go out on the field with him and accept the sectional trophy plaque. *Are you kidding me? With the ball team?* I thought. Heck, what an honor, I sure did! That photo with Tanner, Dad holding the plaque, and me made the local newspaper. How can you be so happy and sad all at once? What a messed up mixture of emotions. *Athens was headed to the state championship.*

A higher power had seemed to be with them that day. The team sensed Tucker's presence, and it was no doubt the team sent a message that they were on a mission. In those two sectional games, Athens scored a total of twenty-four runs. If you recall, I had told the team when they met in our living room the day before to go out and score twenty-five runs. Well, they got pretty darn close to doing just that!

The sectional tournament game wins that day were bittersweet indeed. So many were filled with emotions of grief and sadness for our loss, yet pride for this team and the coaches in their accomplishment. There was enormous heartfelt support for the team and our family from the Athens community.

Following the games, as I was driving back to Athens, my thoughts turned to what Tucker's teammates were going through, going from a high of winning regionals on May 29 and 30, to a low of lows in losing their teammate on June 2, then back to a high of winning sectionals on June 5, and now having to return to another low and attend their teammate's funeral tomorrow. Talk about an emotional roller coaster. Just experiencing the Athens baseball team heading to state alone was enough, but these young kids were having to deal with so much more. This experience and turn of events would leave a lasting impression on each one of them that they would never forget. This was truly an unforgettable time for this entire team. If we all could only imagine what was yet to come. Tucker was much closer than anyone would think.

During the tourney, friends of Tucker were sporting white and blue "Westfall Strong" caps. State qualifier T-shirts were made for the baseball team, which included a baseball heart with Tucker's number 12 and name imprinted on them. The team was going to take Tucker with them every step of the way on this journey.

As the sun went down that day, I cried myself to sleep thinking about the upcoming day—Tuck's funeral.

TRACY WESTFALL

Athens returns to state

Players honor Tucker Westfall during sectional

By Casey Krautkramer

Athens baseball players, coaches and fans have rallied behind Dale and Tracy Westfall this week in the wake of their son, Tucker, dying in a UTV accident on Saturday morning.

Dale, Tracy and their other son, Tanner, walked onto Myron Oatman Memorial Field in White Lake on Tuesday night for the WIAA Division 4 Sectional championship ceremony. The Bluejays easily beat Wausaukee, 10-0, in five innings to advance to the state championships and attempt to defend the state championship they won last season. Athens has a 19-2 record this season.

Tanner Westfall wore an Athens baseball t-shirt with a logo on the front of it in his younger brother Tucker's memory, which includes Tucker's Bluejays baseball uniform No. 12 with wings and a halo. Athens players wore the ironed-on logo in memoriam of their teammate Tucker on their uniform sleeves and hats while they beat Pittsville, 14-1, in five innings in Tuesday morning's sectional semifinal game, and also during the sectional final victory against Wausaukee.

Tucker's white home No. 12 hung on the fence in the Athens dugout during both of its sectional games on Tuesday. Dale Westfall is an Athens varsity assistant coach and he also helps coach the junior varsity team. Tucker Westfall was a freshman this season in the Athens baseball program.

The public address announcer at the White Lake baseball field told Athens head varsity baseball coach Bill Coker to come onto the field to accept the Bluejays' Division 4 sectional championship plaque, but Coker instead allowed Dale Westfall to receive the plaque and hold it up high in front of the Athens players, which surrounded him. Dale Westfall then hugged every Athens player and coach.

Tracy Westfall provided a family statement on the outpouring of support her family has received from the Athens community this week while they grieve the loss of Tucker.

"By now, the sectional games are over and scores are in the scorebook," the Westfall family's statement said. "We have seen the patch worn on the Athens baseball players' uniforms and have been experiencing so many emotions since our loss of Tucker. It is impossible to express how sincerely appreciative we are for this kind gesture.

"To get the best out of our players, they will need to begin by getting the best out of themselves. This team knows how to do that. Although each player has their individual strengths and weaknesses, they have created a deeply rooted sense of togetherness when they go into game mode. It doesn't matter if a player is sitting in the dugout, having to switch up positions on the field, or having a subpar batting day, there always seems to be a sense of unity; now that is powerful. Our family wants to say thank you to the team for commemorating Tucker and touching our hearts in such a special way."

The Athens baseball team united together on Saturday after players heard about their teammate Tucker's death. Local baseball fans were not sure how the Athens players would respond during their sectional semifinal game against a tough Pittsville team on Tuesday. The Bluejays trotted on the White Lake baseball field as a strong-knit family and they trounced the Panthers.

Pittsville hit into two double plays in the first two innings. Panthers starting

See **ATHENS WINS FOR TUCKER/** *page 20*

A SOMBER MOMENT- Athens assistant varsity baseball coach Dale Westfall holds the Division 4 sectional championship plaque high in the air in remembrance of his son, freshman Bluejays baseball player Tucker Westfall, who died in a UTV accident on Saturday morning. Dale Westfall is flanked by his wife, Tracy Westfall, and their sophomore son, Tanner Westfall, during the sectional title ceremony on Tuesday night in White Lake. Athens beat Wausaukee, 10-0, in five innings to give itself a chance to defend the Division 4 state championship it won last season.

#WESTFALLSTRONG

HERE FOR A GOOD TIME, NOT A LONG TIME

CHAPTER 5

The Funeral—June 6, 2018

Dale and I had been looking forward to celebrating this day as it held special significance. Today was our twentieth wedding anniversary.

The significance had now changed and would be forever altered. The memory now was the day of Tucker's funeral. The meaning of this day would never be the same. So much happiness in our hearts just two decades ago has now brought tremendous sadness and a broken heart to each of us. Unbelievable. This was the last day of school for students at Athens High for the 2018 school year. School was scheduled for half a day and Tucker's funeral was planned for the second half to be held in the Athens High School gymnasium.

A decision was made to have Tucker's body cremated with a visitation followed immediately by the funeral. Typically, a visitation would have been held the day before at the local funeral home so family could visit with those who stopped to pay their respects, with the more formal funeral the next day. Our family did not have any interest in going through the standard funeral process. The high school was the only venue most fitting for Tucker. It was the place where Tucker spent his days on the wrestling mat, working out in the weight room, and spending time with friends.

Teachers and staff worked so hard to make this "school" funeral one of the best. The high school was located on the west side of town just off Townline and West Village Limits Road in Athens. It was only minutes from our house.

As one entered the school that day, straight ahead were the heavy weighted gym doors already open. Upon entering the gym, immediately to the right, at the back of the gym were tables covered with crisp white cloths that stood out against the blue background of the school colors. Each table had its own memorial display. Tucker's number 12 baseball jersey was hanging for all to see. On the right was a sign etched on a tall wood slab with bark edging that had a baseball emblem etched with his name and ball number 12 inside of it, with the word *believe* in big bold letters laddered down the entire length of the slab. That same table held his uniformed baseball picture where he had posed with a wide smile holding a bat. The Marawood Conference Championship baseball trophies, the team photos, and his baseball cap and glove were also meticulously positioned on the table. In front of the BELIEVE sign was a football he had kept in his bedroom with a photo of Tucker in his football jersey posing with Dad wearing his coach's shirt.

Tables were set up with blank white memory boards for students and staff to write special messages. A "reflection" table included the annual school photos of Tucker progressing from grade school on up through middle school, a variety of wrestling photos, hunting photos, and photos where he was just hanging out with friends.

Another table displayed Tucker's baby photos and a couple of his baby outfits that I had pulled from a special box at home that was to be given to his bride one day. There were several collages of family vacations, weddings, and so very many with his brother, Tanner, as they were inseparable growing up.

Tucker's letterman jacket, along with other assorted school pullovers that he currently wore were hanging in one display. His large teddy bear dressed in the youth-sized Wisconsin Badgers jacket, which he had outgrown, was propped up on the top of the display as if it was placed there to look up and over all the people in the gym so that he could see Tucker's urn sitting on the table up front. Tucker loved that bear and did not want to get rid of it nor that jacket, so I put the jacket on the stuffed bear, and it laid on his bed. It had been there for years. A red felt banner Tucker made as part of his confirmation requirements at Trinity Lutheran was also on display. On the banner was Tucker's name in white letters down the right side. A little black cross, white dove, and flames decorated the banner in the middle. At the bottom of the banner was part of a quote from Romans 8:26 spiritual reading: "In the same way, the Spirit helps us in our weakness. We do not know what we ought to pray for, but the Spirit himself intercedes for us with groans that words cannot express." This display table was made complete with a second custom-made wood slab imprinted with *#westfallstrong* and the same baseball emblem with his name and ball number inside it.

Around the gym walls were the many rows of blue and white banners displaying Athens High School team and individual conference and state championships for various sports, documenting a proud history of accomplishments.

Looking further into the gym, one could see rows and rows of blue folding chairs set up on the floor, divided in the middle by a good-sized aisle.

Toward the back of the rows where they had run out of blue folding chairs were the older pewter-colored ones. The bleachers were pulled out on each side of the gym as well for additional seating. The school choir would be standing on the bleachers set on the floor at the front of the gym near the stage, later singing certain songs that were planned.

Before entering the center aisle where visitors would later be heading to greet the family stood a small table covered with a blue cloth holding two large wooden boxes. Each box had a beautiful white-tailed deer scene etched on the front. The boxes were open and ready to receive any cards that visitors brought in. A beautiful bouquet of mixed-colored flowers stood between the wooden boxes with a box of tissues strategically placed among a few pens and many blank envelopes.

Dale and I made our way down the middle aisle toward the front of the gym. The dark-blue velvet stage drapes were pulled closed. A large white projector screen was centered on the stage drapes for a video that would be played during the services. The podium where the pastor was to perform the ceremony was just to the right front center of the stage.

I had requested to my family that no one buy flowers, but they didn't listen. There were so many beautiful custom-made floral designs, starter trees, and plants lined up on the floor and arranged on small podiums in front of the stage that it took my breath away. I was in awe in how beautiful this place looked for my dear son.

Centered directly beneath the screen, on the floor in front of the stage, was one more table draped in the school color blue. The framed 5 x 7 photo of Tucker in his prom outfit with Grandpa's gray felt hat, white shirt with black buttons, and maroon suspenders was next to the urn containing his ashes. The urn was most fitting with hunter camouflage colors of brown and orange. Three arrangements surrounded the urn. One arrangement contained a small felt antlered deer and a couple of real deer antlers. Another contained small red and white fishing bobbers among the red roses and bright-yellow carnations. The third arrangement placed behind the urn had a blue ribbon with the word *grandson* on it, with blue, white, and yellow flowers. Another small deer, a small baseball, and blue jay were set among the flowers. A small round memorial stone with a saying entitled "Memories" was placed next to the flower by the urn. Those words read, "What we have once enjoyed we can never lose. All that we love deeply becomes a part of us." Just how many tears can you cry. My sweet son was loved by so many, and it sure was showing.

We had arrived early at the gym, and our parents and relatives (brother, sisters, wives, and husbands) were already milling around, looking at the displays. A small break and snack room were set up for the family just off to the left of the main stage. Once the visitation began, we had no idea there would be no opportunity for even a small break.

Next door to the gym is the school cafeteria. The ladies who normally worked to prepare school lunches were there to help that day. Several long display tables covered with more of those crisp white linen tablecloths were highlighted with blue table runners lined up on the outer walls of the cafeteria. The ladies had set out an amazing display of cookies, bars, cakes, breads, water, coffee, juices, and other refreshments. So many people had baked and contributed. It was just amazing to see. As people completed going through the visitation line, they could come here to visit with others while waiting for the service to begin.

The gym was a large enough venue (*we thought*), until people started coming.

The time had come to start the final process of saying goodbye. Our family of grandparents, aunts, and uncles lined up in the front of the gym by the urn display as visitation began. Dale stood in back by the display tables where you first enter the gym. Tanner and I greeted people about three-fourths of the way up the aisle. We hadn't really a plan, but it worked out quite well this way to spread the visitors out as they arrived.

The baseball team was the first to arrive. Each player was wearing their baseball jersey with khakis. After browsing the displays, they made their way single file down the center aisle to greet us.

There were lines and lines of people coming through after that. It was constant. The hum of voices in the gym grew louder as more people arrived. Our family in the receiving line did their best to console those coming through who were struggling with their own feelings of grief and disbelief. It was so hard and there were so many tears. My heart hurt for them also. This was not going to be easy as I just started to realize how many people interacted with Tucker and our family in some way.

Uncle Tom had arranged for a drone to be flown over the school to capture the number of vehicles parked in the parking lot and down the roadway. We estimated approximately six hundred to seven hundred people were in attendance. None of us in the family had expected this type of turnout. It was an incredible outpouring of support from so many in the local area communities. Opponents Tucker had wrestled over the years had shown up from local towns. Entire sports teams from those in the school conference had showed up. Relatives and friends locally and from outside the Athens area drove in to pay their respects. We had far underestimated what was happening here. It was an overwhelming feeling of love. Many more people continued to come through the line, and it was backing up. The funeral director informed us when it was within a half hour of the funeral service beginning. There was still a line stretched out the gym, which formed two lines in and around the lunchroom, stretching into the front entrance, out the front door, and down the sidewalk. I just knew Dale and I needed to acknowledge all these people. But how were we to accomplish that in the timeframe remaining? So instead of the line coming to us, we left our places and went to them. One by one, we walked through and acknowledged the people standing in line and thanked them for coming. We did try our best to explain why we needed to greet them because of the funeral starting shortly and that we could not engage in much conversation due to the time constraints but were so very grateful they came. Shaking hands, making eye contact, and seeing each and every person was very important to us. We got through the line with just minutes to spare, ending up outside the school on the sidewalk to acknowledge the last of those people who had shown. After returning inside the school, we took our places on chairs in the front row.

The funeral started on time. All those folding chairs and bleachers once empty were filled. The noisy hum of our guests was silenced as the pastor began speaking.

The entire Athens baseball team was seated up front, sitting behind the family in reserved chairs. They were asked to stand and were specially recognized. John Denver's "Take Me Home, Country Roads" and Whitney Houston's version of "I Will Always Love You" were played as the video broadcasted across the stage screen. Tucker had added "Take Me Home, Country Roads" to his playlist on his cell phone after we returned from our vacation to West Virginia. I heard him singing this song while he was showering in our upstairs bathroom one day. The song begins with "Almost heaven, West Virginia…" He was always singing in the shower. I knew this was one song that had to be played today. He was almost in heaven while on our trip in West Virginia. Well, now he is in heaven.

My only regret about the funeral program planning was that I would have requested that the video of Whitney's song not be shown as it was not really appropriate for Tuck's funeral. It was the song that had the meaning. Minor I suppose, but it is something that I had wished was changed. After this song concluded, the student choir sang, and the pastor proceeded with a warm, wonderful, personalized sermon.

Tucker's favorite song growing up was "Ring of Fire" by Johnny Cash. I told Tucker I would be playing that song at his wedding. With deep sadness, this song was now being played to end his funeral. No mom would have ever wanted this to end this way. It was supposed to be a fun and comical wedding, which now would never be.

Friends and family gathered after the service and helped us load up the floral arrangements, trees, and plants. We traveled back to our home for a post-funeral gathering. Many stayed for a short time and left. It was time to rest as this day had taken its toll emotionally for many of us.

That night, I was filled with thoughts of unfulfilled desires. What hurt me the most was that what I wanted for Tucker and what Tucker wanted in life would never be. Number 1 on his to-do list before he died would never be. He would not be able to experience physical love, have a wedding, or have the children and family he had wanted. I too had wanted him to experience what I had and so much more. Now he would never get that chance, and I thought this would bother me the most for the rest of my days.

HERE FOR A GOOD TIME, NOT A LONG TIME

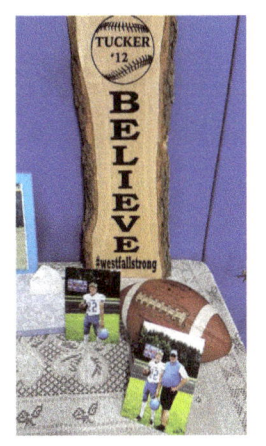

TRACY WESTFALL

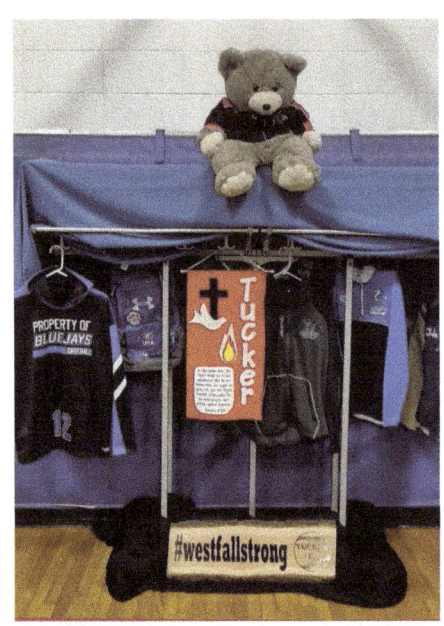

CHAPTER 6

June 7—Shadow

The following day, as crazy as this sounds, I held a garage sale at our home, but it kept my mind occupied. The sale was previously advertised and scheduled as part of the Athens Village Garage Sales being held June 7 through June 9. Other family members had brought in items to sell, and I did not want to disappoint them by not opening up our doors. Many of my items set up and displayed for the sale were not yet marked with price tags. I had planned on marking these items while on my vacation. The reason why items were not marked was explained to people who stopped by to browse. Once they heard why items weren't marked, some actually paid more for items than the suggested amount. Those extra dollars went into Tucker's fund.

My sister Georgine helped me with the garage sale. My sister Wanda dropped by to help with the many flowers that we had brought back from the funeral service the day before. It was a warm, sunny day, so she had taken some of the flower bouquets out onto the front porch to split into smaller vase arrangements. Then later that afternoon, she and a few others walked a couple of blocks down the street to the Assisted Living Apartment Complex and dropped off the floral arrangements for the residents to enjoy. What a beautiful way to share Tucker's memory with more of the community.

That same day, Shadow, Tucker's five-year-old black Pomeranian dog, became ill. He was wheezing, gasping, not eating, and showing difficulty breathing. Dale and I left the garage sale, while other relatives took over, and drove Shadow to the local veterinarian located just a short distance from our house.

Shadow was diagnosed with pneumonia, blastomycosis, and gallstones. He hadn't showed symptoms of being in distress like this the day before. The diagnosis meant multiple surgeries and possible future complications. A family decision was made to put him down.

So a day after Tucker's funeral, we had to say goodbye to Shadow. The way I saw it, no one, no one but Tucker, was going to take care of his dog. He wanted Shadow with him.

Days later, we had a large flat gray stone engraved with the words "Only the Shadow Knows." This was something we would say around our house when unexplainable things happened. It seemed most fitting to have Shadow buried at the front of the firepit entrance in honor of his master. The stone remains today as the stepping-stone to the firepit Tucker wanted in our backyard.

HERE FOR A GOOD TIME, NOT A LONG TIME

ONLY THE
SHADOW KNOWS
2013 - 2018

THANK YOU FOR HONORING TUCKER

CHAPTER 7

Athens High School State Baseball—The Title Win

Athens had won the state baseball championship in 2017 by getting through the semifinal game, beating Oakfield 6–3 and winning the championship game against Independence/Gilmanton 2–0. Coach Westfall (Dad) was an assistant coach on that team. Tucker was still in middle school but looked forward to 2018 when he would hopefully make the team as a freshman. Tanner had decided to go out for track instead that year. Tucker did attend the 2017 game and watched with great anticipation, wanting to be a part of next year's team. Well, he made the 2018 team. He was excited about the possibility that the team had a shot at winning another state baseball championship, and this time he was going to be a part of it. And so, here we are, the team had gotten through sectionals to advance to state. But Tucker wasn't going to be a part of it. Or was he? For Dad, the dream of having coach and son share in a possible championship had vanished. Dad had watched so many coaches and sons over the years enjoy wins together and I'm sure had looked forward to his time with his son, which was now not going to be. Or was it, but in a much different and memorable way?

*****

It was June 13, 2018, just a week after the funeral. I traveled to Fox Cities Stadium in Appleton, Wisconsin. Upon arrival, I received word that a number of players on our baseball team were sick. Apparently, they caught the flu or ate something bad the night before. I looked over at the dugout and the players warming up on the field. They were struggling. Some were throwing up. Players were sprawled out on the benches in the dugout. Oh my gosh, this was not a good sign! I looked over and saw Tucker's number 12 white jersey displayed at one end on the inside of the dugout. Would Tucker be able to give them the incentive they needed? Indeed, I think he did.

*****

Athens was scheduled to play Ithaca first in the semifinal game. Before the game began, both teams met at the infield and knelt, forming a large circle. Everyone bowed their heads. Ithaca's coach said a prayer for Tucker. It was very momentous. Photos of this moment were captured with the game beginning shortly thereafter. There was little action until the sixth inning. I asked Tucker privately for a little magic. Athens scored three runs that inning to win 3–1 to get to the finals. The Athens players left that game exhausted. A few went to get IVs at the local medical facility. Ithaca later received the sportsmanship award for the tournament for that very special historic moment, which took place on the ball field for Tucker.

Athens had once again advanced to the state finals!

The following day a mom and dad shared a story with me. One of Tucker's friends who was in the UTV with Tucker on the day of the accident had slept with his mom and dad at a hotel so they could attend the game the following morning. His friend yelled out at night, "Tucker, we got this!" Both mom and dad heard it clearly and cried. We all wanted that state title!

*****

It was June 14, 2018, state finals day. We had made it. Athens would play the Thorp Cardinals for the 2018 state baseball title, vying for the back-to-back Division 4 state championship.

One of Tucker's girlfriends told me she, her sister, and their dad opened their hotel curtain that morning to see a cloud formation in the form of an eagle feather. They could hardly describe how beautiful it was with the early morning sun casting vibrant orange and yellow rays. By the time they thought to snap a photo, the clouds had shifted, and the formation disappeared.

It was another beautiful day with clear blue sunny skies, no clouds, barely a wind, and comfortable temperatures in the low seventies. The team was feeling better, so whatever bug they had the day before had left their systems. The team warm-ups looked good.

Tucker's white number 12 jersey was again displayed in the dugout. I hadn't been able to talk to Coach Westfall too much as the big game was on the line, but you could feel tension and nerves were high. The team knew what was at stake and appeared prepared to play.

During the playing of the national anthem, a bald eagle captured the attention of the crowd as it was flying nonchalantly above the flags and around the baseball field. Many in the crowd knew from the funeral that Tucker collected little statues of his favorite bird. Was the eagle a sign of foresight and vision of what was about to happen? They can show up when setting your sights on a goal, so maybe this was a special message.

We couldn't help but think Tucker was with us. He was here. I just knew it. As the anthem ended, the eagle made his exit as if to say, "Play ball!"

Marshall Westfall was the starting pitcher and his brother, Connor, was the catcher. Both boys are Tucker's cousins. Javon Penney, another one of Tucker's cousins, was playing right field.

Starting out in the first inning, Marshall hit to center field and got around to third base. Marshall was able to score the first run after Seth Coker grounded out at first. It was 1–0 after the first inning. The Cardinals tied it up in the second and have another run score, so the second inning ends up at 1–2. It was now the top of the third inning. Athens was able to move Klay Ellenbecker around the bases to tie the score at 2–2.

The game moved into the top of the fourth inning. Things became a bit chaotic in a good way. Connor Westfall and Guyler Luther each got on base with back-to-back walks. Javon Penney was up. He bunted the ball down the third baseline. Connor and Guyler advanced to second and third, respectively. Javon outran the throw to first base. Bases were loaded. Excitement was building. Dayne Diethelm was up to bat. The pitch was thrown. Dayne did not swing, but Connor was already halfway from third to home base. Coach Coker had given the sign to run a suicide squeeze! I was thinking, *Can you freakin' believe it?* Coach Coker and the team had used this play a number of times successfully throughout the season, but for it to be successful, the batter needs to bunt or hit the ball as the third base runner is nearly home before the ball gets thrown. If the ball is not hit and caught by the catcher, an out is likely. But now, here they were in the state finals—what a gutsy call!

So what happens? The catcher catches the pitch, stands up, starts a rundown, and throws the ball to the third baseman. Connor was headed toward home plate, turned back toward third, got caught in the rundown, and thrown out by the third baseman. The third baseman then threw to the second baseman to tag Guyler out. Guyler was headed to third. The second baseman made a throw in the rundown to the shortstop (who was then covering third base), but the Thorp shortstop missed the tag on Guyler. The umpire called Guyler safe.

In the meantime, Javon was advancing to second base. The Thorp shortstop threw to the Thorp ballplayer covering second. That player thought Guyler was out and made no attempt to catch the ball. The ball traveled to the outfield. Guyler ran toward home base and scored. Javon ran to third and headed home, scoring from first base due to the overthrown ball. The Athens crowd was going crazy, cheering. Score was now 4–2. But wait, Athens was not done yet! Dayne was still at bat and got on first base after a bobbled error by the third baseman. Colten Weiler was now at bat. There was an overthrow by the catcher to first base, allowing Dayne to advance to second. Colten got walked. Klay Ellenbecker was now up to bat and hit to the pitcher. The pitcher attempted to throw out Colten at second but was in a hurry, and the throw was off. Can you believe it? Bases were loaded again! Four errors by the Cardinal team in a matter of minutes.

Marshall was up to bat and got a base hit, which allowed Dayne and Colten to score. Seth Coker stepped up to the plate. Klay was now on third and scored on a wild pitch. Seth Coker then hit to right field. Marshall was able to come in and score. I'm thinking, *No way! This is wild!* Dakota Willemsen was now at bat and hit to the left field corner. Dakota got a double. Connor was up again. He struck out, making it only two outs. Guyler popped up to the third baseman to end the inning. Score was now 8–2 after only four innings. After scoring six runs in the fourth inning, the side retired. The fans were cheering and breathing a sigh of relief to be ahead with a bit of a cushion.

Between innings, different songs would play loudly over the speaker system. "Ring of Fire" began to play. My eyes opened wide, and my ears were tuned in on the music. Here, right now, in the stadium, in the finals game, after Athens just scored six runs and Thorp had multiple errors. Of all the songs to come across that speaker system, this song was the one that was playing. Tucker's favorite song as he was growing up. It was the song that we had played to end his funeral.

My sister Wanda was sitting next to me. When I heard the first few notes, I grabbed her upper thigh and squeezed it. I could not believe they were playing this song. This song—of all songs! Why? How did they pick it? Tucker knew what had just happened in this inning. Do you think he had something to do with Thorp's errors? Did someone request that this song be played? I cried. Wanda cried. People around us commented about it. I couldn't believe what I was hearing. Did he have something to do with what we all just witnessed—similar to the team pulling out the come-from-behind win at sectionals? I didn't know.

First, the bald eagle flying around during the national anthem; now Tucker's favorite song out of all the songs in the entire universe that could have been selected to play was blaring over the speaker system in the stadium. Many people in the stands had attended the funeral and knew the significance of that song. The pastor had told those in attendance at the funeral. The players on the team heard it and knew the significance of that song. It was all too much to comprehend at that moment.

The Cardinals scored in the bottom of the fourth, and the score changed to 8–5. It was now the top of the fifth inning. Bases were loaded with back-to-back hits by Javon Penney, Dayne Diethelm, and Colten Weiler. No outs yet. Athens was back to the top of the batting order. Klay Ellenbecker was up and hit a long ball to center field, scoring Javon and Dayne easily. Marshall Westfall strategically placed a hit out to center field, and bases were loaded once again. Seth Coker was up to bat. He hit to left field so Colten could score. Score was now 11–5. This was so exciting. This win meant so much to so many.

A second pitching change took place for Thorp. Dakota hit to center field, Klay tagged and scored, and Marshall was thrown out at third. Two outs. Score was 12–5. Dakota Willemssen went in to pitch at the bottom of the fifth inning. The Cardinals threatened with a comeback in the bottom of the sixth inning, scoring five runs. Score is 12–10, getting too close for comfort again, and the nervousness set in. Athens needed to end that Thorp rally!

To my surprise, one more song started to play two innings later. "Broken Halos" by Chris Stapleton was a popular new song, and I would sing along when it played on the radio. That song was also playing on the radio the morning I had driven the boys out to the farm to drop them off to pick rocks the morning of the accident. The last song Tucker would have heard that day. Once again, I was in disbelief and shock. How could this be? How was it possible that a second song that I personally connected with Tucker be playing now at the state finals. I was just sitting there thinking, *he is here!* I knew it. I just knew he was here. He selected this song for me just so I would know he was close. This was just another crazy, emotional day of signs from Tuck.

Athens got one more security run in the top of the seventh. The third out was coming, and the crowd could feel the celebration was near. Thorp failed to score in the bottom on the seventh. Athens won 13–10 and secured a back-to-back state championship!

An on-field celebration started like no other! Cheers, tears, elation! When the third out was caught, Dale and the three other coaches all hugged by the dugout. Dale then ran out to the players who had already started to pile up on each other. He grabbed Connor Westfall, and they made a belly jump onto the pile of players celebrating in the infield. What a moment! Everyone was experiencing waves of happiness and sadness at the same time for the team and coaches. Such a range of emotions—joy, relief, sadness, jubilation, heartache, and so many tears to go with that. It was such a memorable moment for so many.

Talk about a desire to win. What these kids and these coaches just endured the last twelve days… They so much deserved this championship win and certainly have earned it! It was meant to be.

This win with Coach Westfall (Dad) was without Tucker, or maybe not. Was Tucker here the whole time? Coach Westfall (Dad) had to be recognized for his strength in holding himself together through the last few weeks. Coach Coker was instrumental in knowing what to say, how to say it, and when to say it to hold the team together these last couple weeks. I have a deep respect for him, and he should be commended for keeping this team in check. The players on the team were so strong for holding up under their own grief, fighting through illness, and taking an inning at a time to get to their final goal. The players felt Tucker helped them get there. We couldn't see him, but he showed up.

After the game, the local newspaper would quote Seth Coker, "He's always there. We've said since he passed there's ten guys on the field. We're going to beat every team we face because he's always here."

They believed.

This was a win above all wins for this team and their coaches and was exactly what this community needed. This championship win was so, so much more special than what could be put into words. The players and coaches lined up to shake hands with the Thorp Cardinal players. Tanner had pulled Tucker's white jersey and ball pants out of the dugout and carried them through the player's line with him as they all shook hands. The team was awarded their individual medals and team trophy. Tanner accepted Tucker's gold medal. So I guess, in a way, both of Dad's boys were with him on the field for this one memorable moment. And Tucker got his gold medal!

The baseball team returned home victorious. There was a celebratory party at the local VFW building in Athens. I spoke briefly, telling the group that Tucker's number 12 was a representation of what had just been achieved. The number 1 represented the Athens baseball team's win, and the number 2 was a representation of their second state championship. Tucker was along in every way with them. He knew this championship would happen before we did. I wrote this short speech two days before the team won the championship and had been carrying it around in my back pocket, hoping I would be able to say what I had written about the significance of the number 12.

The remainder of the party was lots of fun with many photos with the state trophy and recounting details of the games that had occurred over the past two days. There was reminiscing and camaraderie shared with Coach Bishop and the other players who were part of the 1982 state baseball championship team that Dale had played on.

On June 15, 2018, I contacted the stadium announcer to inquire about the songs that had played between innings. The announcer from the state championship game was at the All-Star Game so I had to wait a few days to hear back from him.

On June 16, 2018, a special fire was lit in the firepit to reflect upon the recent events that happened.

On June 21, 2018, the stadium announcer called me back. I shared my story with him about Tucker, the funeral, and the state baseball game. I asked how the songs that play between innings were selected. He confirmed the songs were preselected and that they had an intern working that day. They often receive song requests on the day of the games but do not accept them. Now, isn't that fascinating that after the inning where Athens scored the most runs that "Ring of Fire" would be the song that got played, then followed with "Broken

Halos"? Of all the songs that could be selected, these two were played. And these songs were *preselected* when Athens played. There were many other divisional games being held that week as well. You can't help but wonder how that happened. Did Tucker know? Did God know and preplan this? You try to make sense of it. You want to wrap your head around it, but you can't. The coincidence of it all is too great, and the odds are astronomical.

*****

Coach Bill Coker was inducted into the Wisconsin Baseball Coaches Association Hall of Fame in February 2019 for his remarkable baseball coaching career. He recorded a 343–125 record, and his teams won nine conference titles, ten regional championships, and had two state championships. It was an honor well deserved.

HERE FOR A GOOD TIME, NOT A LONG TIME

73

TRACY WESTFALL

74

CHAPTER 8

The Impact—Tucker Westfall Memorial

The days that followed were a scene of unification in Athens. Tucker's death had touched this community deeply. The state baseball championship had so many in the community buzzing.

Our family was still numb and elated by all that had happened in just a couple of weeks. However, now it was time to go into action and make good on our promise to place Tucker's funds received from his funeral into the needs of the baseball, wrestling, and football sports programs at the high school.

Uncle Tom had started spearheading efforts to completely transform the Athens High School baseball field. In less than a year, this field would receive a major makeover. The works! The field would be raised to the appropriate levels, with a fresh layer of new field grass, a water basin system, drain tile, underground drainage, an irrigation system, a brand-new scoreboard, in-ground newly framed dugouts with metal siding, new siding on the concession stand/announcer's building, outfield fencing, signs, and topped off with a very special entrance and flagpole area. Dump trucks from area businesses were lined up to haul in around six hundred loads of dirt from Uncle Tom's fields at Miltrim Farms to accomplish this. Businesses with hauling equipment pitched in, contributing their time, manpower, and equipment to help undertake this effort. (See appendix for a detailed list of contributors.)

The target date to have the field transformed was just nine months away before the 2019 baseball season. A remarkable goal was met, and the field was ready to play in April 2019.

Tucker Westfall Memorial Baseball Field dedication ceremony

Before the dedication ceremony, a game was held on April 25, 2019, with Athens playing Phillips. The first pitch was thrown out by Bill Ellenbecker.

The formal dedication ceremony took place on May 3, 2019 (*also Tanner's birthday*). This was truly an accomplishment having this field update completed less than a year following Tucker's death on June 2, 2018. What a tremendous undertaking this community took on to make this happen. This kind of togetherness just doesn't happen everywhere. A culmination of a whole lot of community support brought this beautiful ball field to fruition, and now it can be enjoyed by so many in the years to come. The Westfall family is eternally grateful. It is the Village of Athens's very own "field of dreams."

I took the day off work. It was a beautiful start to the day the morning of the baseball field dedication, with the remainder of the day becoming sunny and partly cloudy with the temperature in the sixty-degree range. Great baseball weather. Approximately four hundred people were in attendance for the dedication ceremony. Dedication brochures were designed and given out. Mini spongy baseball keychains with the T12 logo imprinted on them were handed out as souvenirs. The shed housing the school vans had been transformed into a beautifully decorated time space of photos showing the project from the beginning up to the very end. Z99 WIGM in Medford broadcasted the game, as did another broadcasting network out of the Marshfield area, Zaleski Sports. Camera crews and reporters from the news stations for Channel 9 and Channel 7 were also present to do stories for their evening broadcasts. Players were interviewed from our team. Athens ended up defeating their opponent, Edgar, 16–6 in six innings, making this a special end to a very special day for the Westfall family and the Bluejay team.

HERE FOR A GOOD TIME, NOT A LONG TIME

Two baseball bollards invite you to walk down to the field on a newly poured concrete sidewalk leading to the field. About three fourths of the way down the path, a bronze bust of Tucker is displayed on top of a white marbled stone patterned like a home plate. In front of the bust, resting on the plate is a bronze plaque with Tucker's lasting legacy for others to follow. It reads, "We are all here for a good time! Greet each other with a smile and enjoy the game." Next to the plaque is a bronze baseball. The plate rests on a large rock donated by a local business. On the side of the rock is a bronze honorary sign thanking the many businesses and citizens for making this possible. A flagpole located near the ball field was donated by the American Legion and VFW and carries special meaning. Below the American flag is a bald eagle flag in honor of Tucker. At the ceremony, a custom metal work baseball sign was unveiled with TUCKER WESTFALL MEMORIAL FIELD etched in a large baseball. This young man now officially has a baseball field named in his honor. What is even more significant—he knows it!

Following the game, the Westfalls invited anyone who wanted to, to come downtown to a local establishment for complimentary refreshments as a way to share in our family's gratefulness to the many persons involved in making this project possible.

*****

Following the renovation of Tucker's field, certain significant events have happened.

On May 29, 2019, Seth Coker hit the first home run at Tucker Westfall Memorial Field during the regional finals game against Edgar. Athens won 15–7. This was extra special given Seth was the first student honored with the Tucker Westfall Memorial Scholarship.

On May 19, 2021, Cooper Diedrich hit a home run out of Tucker's ballpark. The wind was right; the hit was solid. Cooper and Tucker lifted weights in the weight room growing up and spent a lot of time hanging out together. Cooper was just one of many special friends to Tucker.

On June 22, 2021, the first sectionals tourney playoffs were held at Tucker Westfall Memorial. I woke up to a large blue jay in our feeder. He flew across the street to the neighbor's tree and looked back. I really think Tucker was there to greet me and knew exactly what this day meant. Throughout the day, I received many compliments about the ball field and the grounds. Team photos were taken as memories of the day as well as me introducing myself as Tucker's mom and wishing the players and coaches the best of luck in advancing to the state tourney.

HERE FOR A GOOD TIME, NOT A LONG TIME

August 8, 2018

Athens' own Field of Dreams

Construction of a new Athens High School baseball field is going smoothly so far. Dean Ellenbecker, president of S.D. Ellenbecker, Inc., said his work crew, shown in the background last Wednesday, has finished pouring the concrete foundation for the baseball dugouts, which are four feet into the ground. His crew still needs to pour the concrete roof on the dugouts, after the wood dugout frames are completed. S.D. Ellenbecker has also installed drainage tiles underneath the baseball field. Dean Ellenbecker and many other businesses in Athens are donating their work crews for the baseball field project, including Janke General Contractors, Switlick & Sons and Miltrim Farms. Dean Ellenbecker said several individuals are also donating their time working on the ballfield project, including his retired brother, Bill Ellenbecker, Bill Yessa and Bob Liss, just to name a few. Dean Ellenbecker anticipated the grass seed would be planted sometime this week in the outfield, to allow it enough time to grow and be ready for the 2019 spring baseball season.

TRACY WESTFALL

HERE FOR A GOOD TIME, NOT A LONG TIME

TRACY WESTFALL

HERE FOR A GOOD TIME, NOT A LONG TIME

TRACY WESTFALL

HERE FOR A GOOD TIME, NOT A LONG TIME

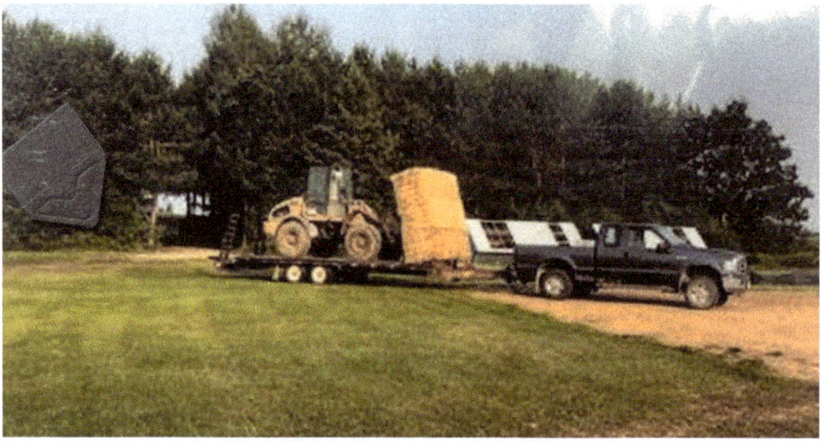

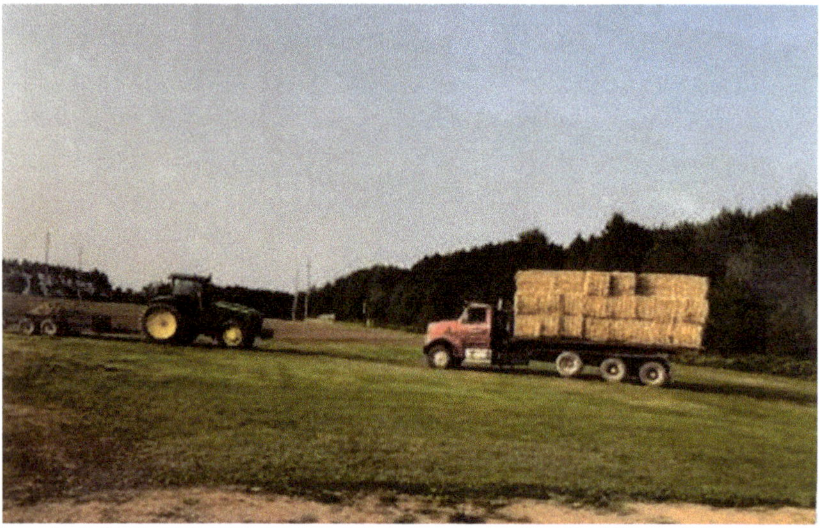

HERE FOR A GOOD TIME, NOT A LONG TIME

TRACY WESTFALL

HERE FOR A GOOD TIME, NOT A LONG TIME

TRACY WESTFALL

HERE FOR A GOOD TIME, NOT A LONG TIME

Watering For New Field Grass

TRACY WESTFALL

HERE FOR A GOOD TIME, NOT A LONG TIME

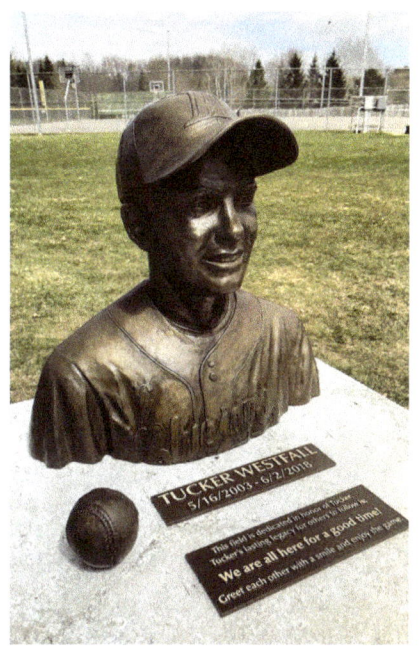

CHAPTER 9

The Psychic

I was struggling with dealing with Tucker's death and wanted questions answered. I had seen the shows on TV of psychics and how they could connect with the spiritual world. Could this happen between Tuck and me? Well, I wasn't sure but felt it important enough for my self-being that I needed to explore this avenue. I was apprehensive but so wanting to have certain answers. I have only heard about being able to connect with the spiritual world, wondering if I could really connect with Tucker.

We (Tucker and I) researched the internet on my cell phone together while I sat on the bed in his room. Lori Ann Mans, a renowned psychic who works in Appleton, Wisconsin, kept popping up in my mind, and I continued to go back to her website. The decision was made—she was the one, so I booked a reservation for Monday, December 17, 2018. I told Tucker I wanted and needed some answers, and he needed to come to this lady and talk to me. I just had to find out if this really works. Eager with anticipation and yearning of the possibility of being able to connect with Tucker in some way was exciting. I continued to prepare him as the weeks, days, and date got closer by talking to him daily in his room, letting him know what I was going to do. As I traveled down to Appleton on December 17, I was letting him know today was the day and not to be afraid and come forth. I got more than I bargained for.

HERE FOR A GOOD TIME, NOT A LONG TIME

When I got to Ms. Mans's office, I parked my vehicle on curb side parking and walked to the address. The building was an older historic-looking hotel. Inside was an elevator with a solid intricate mass of beautifully carved metal. Checking further as I was waiting for the elevator, I found her office listed on the second floor. Once the doors opened, I stepped inside and was taken to the second floor. Her office was located just outside the elevator door. I walked inside and found a middle-aged woman sitting there. She invited me in while having a bite to eat between sessions. Ms. Mans introduced herself. She had me sit on a couch in a small room and instructed me to answer "yes or no" to her questions. Ms. Mans did the talking. Before starting, I asked if I could videotape her. She responded I could not but that I could record her words. I was so nervous I could not locate the recorder on my cell phone, so Ms. Mans assisted me.

Here we go. No words were exchanged. Within moments of her beginning the session, she started chuckling. She described this young boy that had come forth. She went on to say that he was a joy to be around. He was fun and had a quick wit about him. She repeated that he was just a joy to be around.

She started to describe a female who was with this boy, showing him around (in heaven). She first described her as a friend, then a relative, and then started detailing how she had died of cancer and worked at a medical facility. I put it together that this must be my cousin, Kristle Snyder, whom Ms. Mans was referring to. We lost Kristle on August 23, 2014, after a battle with cancer. She was only forty-nine years old then. One would say Kristle and I mirrored each other in many ways growing up. We were born the same year, married the same year in 1998, and had two boys nearly the same ages. My boys were born in 2002 and 2003; Kristle's boys were born in 2001 and 2002. Kristle worked in the medical field and cared for so many. She was a petite, beautiful-looking girl with the kindest of hearts. Ms. Mans went on to say she knew T-shirts were made for Kristle by those who worked with her following her death. I later confirmed there were T-shirts made by her medical friends. Kristle wanted me to know, saying (through Ms. Mans), "I got your boy!" If I ever wanted someone to care for Tucker, it would definitely be

Kristle. I knew then he was in good hands as Kristle was one of the kindest, sweetest, and most loving people on earth you would ever meet. Everyone in our extended family had adored her. It was comforting to know Tucker was receiving guidance from her. I later shared this information with Kristle's mom and dad (my aunt and uncle) and Kristle's husband.

Ms. Mans continued the session by pointing out some things only our family would know about. For example, Tucker told his brother to stay out of his room. It was how Ms. Mans heard Tucker say it and how she relayed that message with the expression in her voice that made this unique, as I could definitely hear Tucker saying it that way. Recall, I had mentioned earlier how very protective he was of his room and the items in it.

Ms. Mans went on to say that Tucker wanted to acknowledge his aunts and uncle *(my sisters and brother)*. He specifically singled out Aunt Lorene, as she has her birthday close to the same date as his in the month of May. There were more family details shared that only Tucker or our family would know about. I was very attentive to all she was sharing.

The recorded session with Ms. Mans went on for about one hour. Tucker made a comment that raised my attention even more. He said (through Ms. Mans), "You wouldn't believe it. You just wouldn't believe it." It was both of our beliefs that he was talking about heaven and could not put into words how to describe it. Tucker went on with trying to relay information about the symbols and letters and how he recognized they were about him, designed in honor of him. Ms. Mans did not have a clear vision on what he was trying to relay, but I knew. He was referring to the car stickers—the T12 and T22 designs. He knew about the people talking about him via microphones and that it was ongoing. Ms. Mans stated she hadn't seen such recognition like this before. "And it's continuing," she said. "It's ongoing."

I know this to be true as Tucker was recognized at his annual golf outing, the 2018 graduation ceremony, and the 2019 baseball field dedication. Microphones were used at each of these events. Ms. Mans said Tucker turned sideways and showed her that he had one wing (*a guardian angel wing*) and that he was working on getting the other wing.

We here on earth certainly wouldn't know what one would have to do in the afterlife to receive a second wing, but I'm sure Tucker has worked and earned that wing by now and that I have a guardian angel watching over me. Ms. Mans went on to say that in her many years of conducting readings, she had maybe come across less than five people who had their wings. Just goes to show you how special Tucker really was here on Earth.

There were a few questions I still had, so I went ahead and asked to see what kind of response I'd get. I wanted to know why Tucker set up his Instagram motto the way he did. Recall, it read, "Here for a good time, not a long time." He responded that I was reading too much into it. (Well, I had to ask, and he's not here now.)

Then I asked what Tucker was doing now that he was in the spirit world. Ms. Mans closed her eyes briefly and then went on to report that Tucker was in this very large amphitheater. Children of all ages were seated throughout the area. Tucker was one of the oldest and tallest of the children seated in the group and stood out in the back of the amphitheater. He was listening to this guy who was up in front. After that guy was done speaking, everyone kind of went away.

She stated Tucker was then back at our home and hung with the family. He heard us, listened to us, and knew what was going on. He saw the words I wrote about him (like I have done for years in preparation for writing this book). She said Tucker said, "Don't worry, Mom, I always hear you." There was a segment where details of the accident were discussed. Tucker did know that his friends were okay following the accident. She mentioned how certain people were making it look to be that Tucker was to blame, but his hands were not as dirty as people were trying to make it out to be. There were other things that happened. This information was part of the investigation that followed the accident and for purposes of this book, I will not go into detailed facts of the accident.

After leaving this personal reading, my head was spinning about how much she got spot-on about my situation, what happened, and our family. This was one of the most fascinating events I have ever experienced. I listened to that recording again and again so I could absorb all she had covered in such a short amount of time. That reading was much more than I had ever imagined. I felt relieved. Relieved that Ms. Mans provided substance that supported the information I was seeking. Relieved that Tucker was near. She nailed his character, his charm, his ways. It felt like Tucker was leaning right over her shoulder, translating information to me. She brought up details that only those close to Tucker would know. I had received validation and reassurance that Tuck was, in a way, really still with us, only now in a spiritual way. This had forever changed how I view the afterlife. I still talk to Tucker, and he still lets me know he's around.

I shared the recording with Dale, Tanner, and both our families on Christmas Eve. I pondered about whether this was the right time as the loss was still hitting the families very hard. I did not know how this information would be received because I did not tell anyone what I was doing. No one had an idea until I played the recording that Christmas Eve. My hope was that, although it was something very different that no one in our family had ever experienced, in the end they would be glad I shared the recording. It was my further hope that they went away with a renewed and more open awareness that there is life after death. Tucker, as well as many others we have lost over the years, did want to reach out, and he really knows what is going on and watches over us. Growing up in our family, this type of subject would never be talked about as our family was very reserved on expressing themselves in such a way. This had to have broadened their views about death and heaven. In a good way, when I continued to share "happenings" with my mom and dad and told them I just couldn't make this stuff up, they did seem more accepting of life after death in a way I never thought they would.

CHAPTER 10

The Autopsy

On January 17, 2019, I picked up a compact disc (CD) containing the autopsy photos and report from the coroner's office.

Taking time to prepare myself for what I was about to see, I started viewing the CD. The first thing I noticed was his underwear. I thought, *Wait, I saw Tucker in brown underwear in the ambulance. These photos show him in blue-gray underwear. How can this be?* I am positive of what I saw because I had shared certain details with others and mentioned the brown underwear. As I looked further, I did not see Tucker in the ambulance the way Tucker was in the photos. I did not see the abrasion on his face and cheekbone. Either the EMS personnel did a very good job on him before I saw him, or did the Lord, or Tucker, not want me to see him in a certain way and placed a nearly perfect, uninjured body vision in front of me to protect me? I do not know. I was perplexed but still reflected back and was certain of what I saw. I just could not believe the underwear color and that I was seeing different markings on his face from what I recall seeing while I was in the ambulance on the day of the accident.

Continuing on in reviewing the photos, it was obvious to me he was thrown from the UTV and skidded across the gravel driveway. His lower right arm did not have any abrasions on it, so it appears he was protecting his face by shielding it with his forearm. There was a slight abrasion scraping on his right cheek. His right shoulder was reported to be dislocated, which led me to believe his shoulder hit hard against the corner of the UTV rooftop, or it hit the ground when he was ejected from the UTV. Miscellaneous scratches were going in different directions on the right side of his chest area, which was likely caused from coming in contact with weeds at the side of the driveway where the culvert was. At some point, the back right side of Tucker's head was hit, causing the life-ending head injury he suffered. A few feet one way or another and Tucker might still be here. We can all only accept what has happened. Additional scrapes were on his upper and mid back area. His left arm was heavily discolored and was a deeper red than the normal skin color.

    These were difficult photos to view, but necessary for me to bring closure and a full understanding of what Tucker might have gone through. It is hard to reflect and envision what your child may have been going through each second, each moment, until the end. It still brings so many tears and sadness. You want things to be different, realizing, though, you must accept what has happened.

CHAPTER 11

Special Moments

This chapter is a collection of special moments that have taken place that consistently remind me that Tucker is near.

September 10, 2018. I called it a "Monday Mourning." Eugene Denk brought over a bronze eagle that he had kept, telling me it was likely more than a hundred years old. He gifted it to me in honor of Tucker. If you recall, Eugene was one of the last people to speak with Tucker while he visited with him on our porch the evening before the accident. I wanted to display this eagle with Tucker's bust at the ball field but later decided not to place it there in fear of it being taken. It has a safe place in our home.

December 2, 2018. It was Dale's fifty-third birthday and six-month anniversary of Tucker's death. It was a very tough day emotionally. Five of Tucker's friends and their parents showed up at our door bringing with them a beautiful pink and white carnation bouquet for me, and evergreen Christmas boughs in a box. They also brought venison jerky, brownies, balloons, and two very special ornaments sporting footballs and blue jays. It was one of those very special moments when friends and parents gathered, thinking both of Tucker and caring about his dad. One of Tuck's friends showed me his class ring that had Tucker's name specially engraved on the inside.

January 2019. In addition to the baseball team ties that Tucker had, the wrestling community had also been affected by Tucker's death. The Tomahawk coach, wrestlers, and community presented a five hundred-dollar check to Coach Dale at the dual wrestling meet held in Athens. The money was used for wrestling backpacks for the wrestlers to carry their shoes, singlets (one-piece, tight-fitting uniforms), and change of clothes to away matches and weekend tournaments.

January 24, 2019. It was Wrestling Parents Night at Athens. Athens had a wrestling dual with Chequamegon. Long-stemmed white roses were given out to recognize all the parents and as a symbol of peace and remembrance of Tucker.

January 26, 2019. Conference wrestling was held at Auburndale. Before the start of the finals matchups, Dale was awarded the Jerry Hahn Memorial Award, a prestigious award given to someone in the wrestling family who has devoted themselves, gone above and beyond, and is recognized as a longtime member of the wrestling family.

These are difficult wrestling gatherings to attend as I would much rather be watching Tucker hanging with all his wrestling buddies from the bleachers. I sat in the stands in kind of a stupor, waiting for the final round to begin, then suddenly recognized a familiar voice start talking over the speaker system. He was an Athens alumni and wrestling coach standing on a mat in the middle of the gym floor, talking through a microphone. He was reading from a piece of paper and started saying: "Wrestling runs deep in the heart of the Westfall family. Dale was a senior in 1984 when Athens won its first State Team Championship, and Dale was a state runner-up himself in 1984. Dale went on to coach wrestling at Wild Rose after college and then came back to be head wrestling coach in Athens in 2007, where he has coached twenty Athens state qualifiers at State." It started to sink in what was happening. I looked over to Dale who was mat side with his wrestlers, leaning up against the school's concrete wall. He started to tear up. The alumni member continued: "Dale and Tracy had two boys, Tanner and Tucker, who were wrestlers. In June 2018, Tucker lost his life in a tragic UTV accident. With the support of many families and friends, the Westfall family persevered through tragedy and brought everyone closer together. Dale is the type of guy who would give the shirt off his back and is always there when you need him. He is passionate with helping kids and gives back to the community. His wife, Tracy, and son, Tanner, are always by his side and support each other. Dale's dedication and passion for the sport of wrestling is second to none."

I cried. He cried. Although this honor was all for Coach Westfall, I was asked to come down from the bleachers onto the mat to join Coach Westfall in receiving this award. It was another one of those very emotional moments. The gym erupted in congratulatory claps as Dale accepted the award. I was so proud of him in all he had done for the wrestling program and his wrestlers over the years, at the same time thinking Tuck should be here because it was Dad's time to coach his own son. And for those who knew Dad and Tucker, one couldn't help to think that many of those words spoken mirrored the kind of young man his son was becoming and would have grown to be like, as he had already been walking in Dad's shoes.

February 21, 2019. The wrestling season continued and once again Coach Westfall had coached three more Athens state qualifiers. At 8:00 a.m., a pep rally was held to send the kids off to state. One wrestler was Tucker's cousin, which made it even more special. Dale started to speak at the rally and say how proud he was of these guys, then choked up. He had to step away with tears. This was all too emotional and just too soon yet following Tucker's death. There was one key wrestler not present to take part in, or be part of, this send-off. One could feel that Tucker was there to see and hear this, and I sensed the wrestlers so wanted him to be there. Following the rally, the coaches and wrestlers left the school and caravanned down to state for the tournament.

February 24, 2019. Lorene texted me early Sunday morning, asking me to check out a state wrestling article that she just read in the newspaper. It had Dale and Tucker's cousin commenting about Tucker while at the wrestling state tourney and the effect this was still having on them. I have included this article as part of the book. It continued to be an extremely emotional time for our family.

A couple of days after the state wrestling tournament ended, I traveled back to Madison to attend a sales meeting for the insurance company I work for. So many supportive people from the company were asking how our family was doing. I shared Tucker's recording with one of the insurance agents whom I work closely with and was given a "Wings of Change" bracelet. My thoughts returned to Tucker having a wing in heaven and working to earn the other.

Mid-June 2019. Another garage sale was held. A year had gone by now. Dale's mother shared with me a spiritual encounter which she had with her own dad after he died. She had never told anyone because she didn't want one to think she was crazy. She was sitting in her recliner and a light beam came toward her. She heard her dad say in his male voice, "Marlene, I love you." Sharing this encounter with me meant so much because I had shared the recording and other happenings with her, not knowing if others had experiences such as mine. It was comforting that she could share her experience with me.

A lady stopped by the garage sale with her two boys that day and spoke about the model airplane kits I had for sale. She told her boys to each select one kit. I asked if I could take the boys upstairs and show them the finished look of the little model airplanes we had already done so they would have an idea of what they would look like. She and the boys came inside our home as she asked how I was doing. She knew Tuck's story. The conversation continued as I shared with her that I talk to Tuck, that he has come to me in dreams, and described things I have experienced. She proceeded to tell me her own story about seeing her brother's death due to an airplane crash and the grief she has gone through for years. Her uncle had been flying the plane and it nose-dived, killing her brother. Her uncle survived. She has struggled for fifteen years with intense grief and traumatization from seeing her brother die in that crash and finally needed to seek therapy to cope.

I tried to share these stories with Dale, but he was not very empathetic. He wanted to change the subject and asked about a bruise on his chest. I wanted him to listen and care and wished he would believe so he could experience some of what I have. He seemed like he was internalizing his feelings. I wanted him to talk more, but he just didn't. It is my opinion that many people want to share their stories but don't want to be thought of as crazy or weird. Well, I support them and realize what is happening to me is not crazy or weird and that these people are not either. I am interested in hearing their stories and not interested in keeping the experiences that have happened to me to myself. These things that are happening need to be shared.

Late July 2019. Dale told me that sectionals baseball tournament for 2020 would be hosted at the Tucker Westfall Memorial Field in Athens. What an honor for Tuck!

September 2, 2019—the first day of school for Tanner as a senior and what would have been the first day for Tucker as a junior. When I got up that morning, on the porch was a card and a mum from a very special mom in the area. The card read, "You matter." She, a mom herself, was thinking of this mom today. How thoughtful and caring this was, as it was another milestone morning. This was a very special time for these kids, and Tuck's not here to enjoy it with his friends. Plenty of tears flowed today.

Mid-December 2019. Tony Thurs stopped by to give the Westfall family one thousand dollars in funds raised from his "Moving the Needle" college project. Beyond awesome! This is what we continue to see in this small, giving community. It has been over a year and a half since Tucker's death, and yet so many people are still affected by the loss of him. It has become a real eye-opener to realize how many, young and old, have been impacted by Tucker's death.

September 2020. Tucker's friends start their senior year in high school.

October 1, 2020. Tucker's classmate and friend asked if I would join the football team on the field when they announce and recognize the seniors on Senior Night at the start of tomorrow night's game. They wanted Tucker's name announced. They didn't have to ask me twice. Of course, I was so honored to be asked. I knew how much this would mean to him to be out there with his teammates one last time. I arrived at the football game. Not only was it Senior Night, but it was also Homecoming. Large blown-up photos of the senior football players were posted up on the building where one would pay to enter the game. Tucker's photo was on top. After the national anthem, the seniors were called out to the field one by one. Lastly, they called Tucker Westfall. I walked out to the fifty-yard line wearing his number 22 jersey to greet the entire team. They were all clapping as I approached. I got very emotional and told the team, "I love you, guys! Kick some ass tonight." The words were sudden and spontaneous. I didn't know where they came from…well, maybe I did. It would have been something Tucker would have said. I turned and left the field and stood on the sidelines to watch the game. Tucker did what he asked with Athens winning the game that night against Thorp 56–8. What a coincidence that, if one recalls, Thorp was once again the opponent here as Athens played them in the state baseball championship. What a night to remember. The game was even viewable on YouTube on the following link: This evening's Homecoming Football game Thorp at Athens will be broadcast on: https://www.youtube.com/channel/UCTCCf1oyUnV2tkaGV2DCgLg/live.

October 24, 2020. After the football game between Athens and Stevens Point Pacelli, a few parents approached me, asking me to stick around and come out to the field after the game. A fairly large group of parents and students grouped in a semicircle around us. The senior football players strolled in, standing next to and behind Dale and me. An autographed photo of Tucker was presented to us. It was the same large photo of Tucker that was on display for Senior Night, but now all of the seniors had signed it. They also presented us with a senior photo of the players sitting on a bench with Tucker screened in on the background. A life-size football with Tucker's picture and his jersey number 22 imprinted on it was also given. I was touched so deeply. I told the group about Tucker having footballs and baseballs autographed and on display in his room, so for his friends who meant the world to him to have the photo autographed was truly special beyond words. Today, these items remain displayed in his room. They will hold special meaning for the rest of my life. What was interesting was I, too, had a surprise for the senior players. Remember Senior Night when I walked out onto the field. Well, I had a card specially made of a photo of me walking out to the football players on the field. A note inside the card thanked them for letting me walk in Tucker's shoes on the football field with them (his buddies) one last time. A photo of Tucker in his jersey from the last year he played with his buddies was also enclosed as a keepsake. It was just another emotional time, another emotional day.

December 2020. I was contacted by one of the students working on the high school class annual. The senior class wanted to dedicate their annual to Tucker and needed photos. The next few days, I spent laying out photo albums and tagging certain school-related photos of Tucker throughout his fifteen years that might be chosen to use. This was another one of those tough but necessary times to go through. There was a lot of crying that day. His classmate came to my house and went through the albums, pulling photos that she thought would work well.

Mid-January 2021. I took one of Tucker's T-shirts over to Mrs. Westfall to be included in a graduation quilt she was having made for her daughter. Tucker had cut the sleeves on this shirt shortly before he died because he wanted to wear it and show off his muscles. "Sun's out, guns out," he would say. The quilt was made for her daughter, also Tucker's cousin, who would have graduated with him in May of 2021. My mom handstitched Tucker's signature on the shirt to add a little something extra that no one else had and ironed a number 12 on it. This was a one-of-a kind special remembrance for a very special cousin.

February 11, 2021. The Athens boys basketball team won a conference title after seventy-two years. It was a momentous night. Afterward, players and coaches on the team cut down the nets; one went on the trophy, and the other net was pieced up as a keepsake for each player. Two of Tucker's senior basketball friends saw me hanging around after the game. Each one approached me separately and gave me a hug, thanking me for coming to watch. I couldn't help but cry because history was made, and Tucker was not here to share it with them. It hurt so. There were few words that needed to be exchanged as they both knew what I was thinking.

In February 2021, Dale shared a story with me that happened at school. The flags were flying at half-mast, and he asked his fifth-grade student why. The student thought for a moment and asked, "Is it Tucker Westfall Day?" Dale smiled and answered, "It is not." What a nice sentiment. He thought I'd enjoy that one.

January 22, 2022. The Athens wrestling team held a raffle after the Athens youth wrestling tournament at the school. Our family helped out by Dale and I working the clock and scoring the brackets. Tanner got a workout being a ref for the kindergarten matches. Dale had bought two fifty-dollar raffle tickets a couple of weeks before the tournament. He put a mailing address label on one ticket and hand-wrote his name on the second ticket, saying, "I bought you a ticket. Yours is the one with the address label on it." Well, the ticket with the address label on it was pulled for the one thousand-dollar prize. It just so happened Dale and I were helping bartend at a retirement party held at the Miltrim Farms new visitor center that evening, so we weren't at the Landmark Bar when they pulled the winners for the 8:00 p.m. drawing. It took two days to find out for sure that the winning ticket pulled had the address label on it.

So don't tell me someone's not listening and making things happen. I do have a guardian angel!

HERE FOR A GOOD TIME, NOT A LONG TIME

Bronze Eagle From
Mr. Denk

Athens wrestlers find inspiration from fallen teammate

Mike Sherry
Wausau Daily Herald
USA TODAY NETWORK - WISCONSIN

MADISON – Almost nine months have passed since Tucker Westfall's life was cut short at age 15 in a UTV crash while heading to a farm near his Athens home. His family, friends and the Athens community will never forget that tragic June 2 day, and while there are good moments, there are still plenty of times when the emotions are difficult to deal with.

The WIAA state individual wrestling tournament this weekend at the Kohl Center was one of those times.

"It's hard to be here," Dale Westfall said, choking back tears. "I haven't dealt with it very well, as you can see."

Dale, who is Tucker's father, is the wrestling coach at Athens High School and Tucker was an aspiring wrestler as well as a baseball and football player.

Athens qualified four wrestlers for the state tournament, including junior Connor Westfall, who is Tucker's cousin. Connor said he thinks about Tucker for motivation and inspiration every time he steps on the mat.

"Tucker's dad is our head coach and his wife (Tracy) came in probably our second day of practice and she explained to us (Tucker's) goals," Connor said. "We have a pep rally at our school and his mom said he would have wanted to be sitting on the stage in the state qualifier chairs."

Dale Westfall was also an assistant coach on the Athens baseball team, and Tucker's cousins Marshall and Connor Westfall and Javon Penney were key players for the Bluejays. Less than two weeks after Tucker's death, they paid tribute to their late freshman teammate by winning the team's second consecutive state baseball title. Tucker's jersey was hanging in the Athens dugout at Fox Cities Stadium in Grand Chute. In July, the community held a golf tournament at Black River Golf Club in Medford to help raise money to renovate the Athens baseball field in honor of Tucker.

"We put up a new baseball field this year, Tucker Westfall Memorial," Connor said. "Our whole town has just been emotional. Very emotional."

Dale Westfall, who said some of the money from the golf outing was also used to buy new uniforms for the wrestling team, said the outpouring of support for his family and for the Athens wrestling team this weekend has been

See WRESTLERS, Page 4D

4D ‖ SUNDAY, FEBRUARY 24, 2019 ‖

Wrestlers
Continued from Page 1D

heartwarming.

Fighting back tears again, he wanted to let everyone know it is appreciated.

"It's very big. It's a big deal," he said.

TRACY WESTFALL

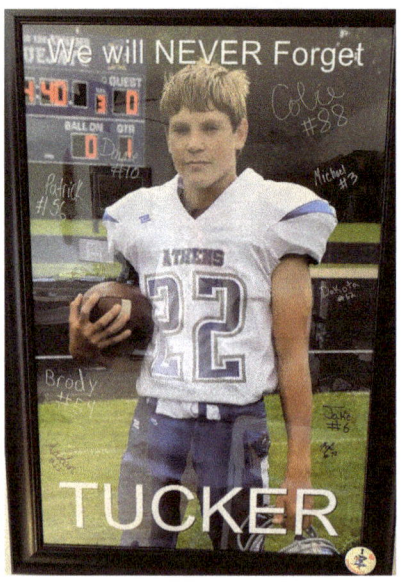

Autographed Photo By Senior Football Players

HERE FOR A GOOD TIME, NOT A LONG TIME

Football Presented To Our Family

TRACY WESTFALL

FOR ONE LAST TIME

I KNOW YOU COULDN'T SEE ME, BUT I WAS THERE.
I WAS WALKING ON THE FIELD THROUGH MY MOM'S FOOTSTEPS.
THE WORDS SHE SPOKE WERE MINE.
YOU DID WHAT I ASKED AND MADE
 SENIOR DAY AND HOMECOMING MEMORABLE.
I WATCHED OVER YOU AND SAW WHAT YOU DID.
I WILL NEVER FORGET THAT YOU INCLUDED ME –
THAT I COULD BE WITH THE TEAM MEANT EVERYTHING TO ME . . .

FOR ONE LAST TIME!

Tucker

HOMECOMING & SENIOR DAY 2020
ATHENS -56 THORP - 8

HERE FOR A GOOD TIME, NOT A LONG TIME

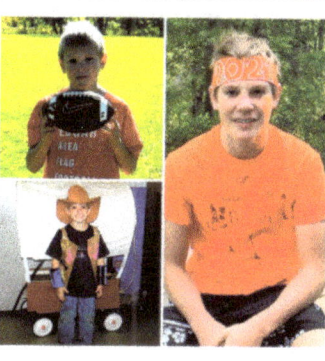

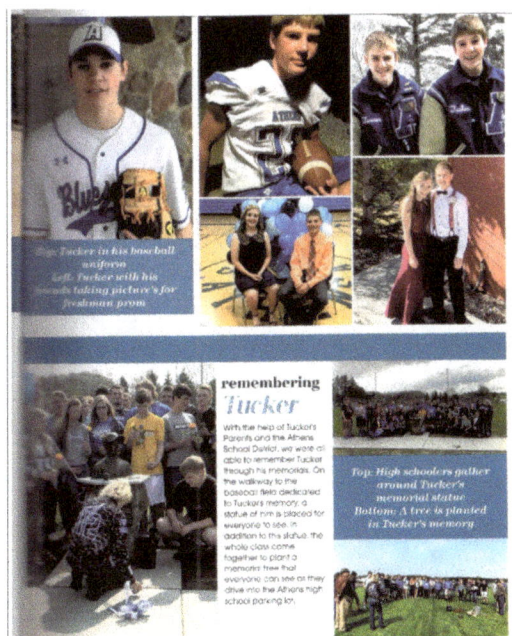

Class Annual Dedication Page

113

TRACY WESTFALL

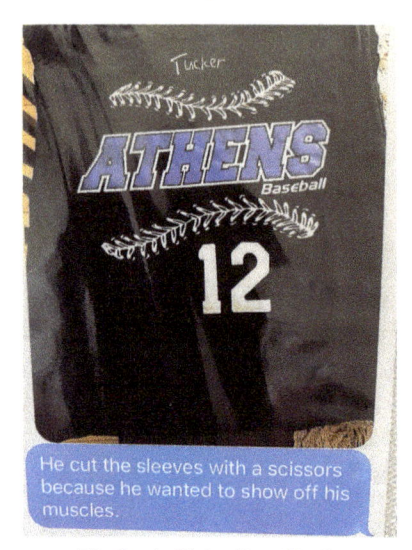

Tucker's Shirt For Quilt

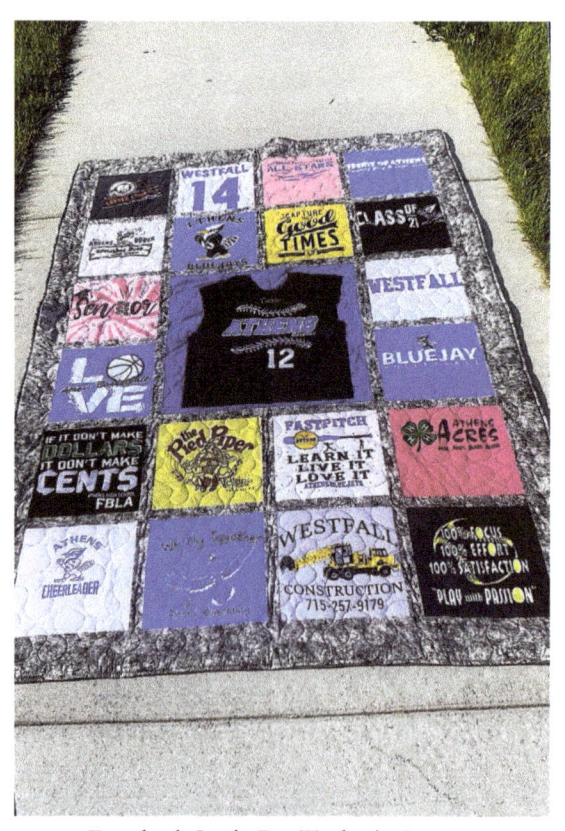

Finished Quilt For Tucker's Cousin

CHAPTER 12

So Many Signs

The days, months, and years following Tucker's death, I kept a diary of signs that I could not dismiss with a feeling that he was near, trying to comfort me and my family. Bald eagles were frequently seen sitting on trees near the roadside, flying overhead, and flying at me. This did not happen before; that's what was so interesting. There were also numerous blue jay sightings (near the firepit, in the woods where I hunt, in nearby trees, crossing my path when driving to places I visit, or just flying nearby in my view). Baby frogs started to appear after I decided to keep a small red frog Tucker wanted to sell at the next garage sale.

Below are dates and a summary of happenings that I felt were worthwhile sharing in this book. There are so many more, so I have highlighted certain ones. Tucker visits in my dreams, and I encourage him to visit. What is great about that is I get to see him in ways no one else can. It really is a beautiful thing. Call it timing, coincidence, or just a circumstance, but I'm sure if one is open to it, you, too, may have received signs from loved ones who have passed and can relate to these types of similar experiences. One should know they are not alone. These are very special happenings with me, and there is but one spirit and soul behind it… Tucker.

June 19, 2018—Cleaning up after garage sale. A perfect yellow monarch was on the concrete floor in the garage. I placed it in a special box in Tucker's room where it still can be seen in pristine condition.

June 29, 2018—Dale attended the Oshkosh All-Star high school baseball games. Afterward, he, a parent, and another coach went to Ground Round near the riverfront. They got out of the vehicle and started walking toward the restaurant. A band across the river was playing "Ring of Fire." It was only weeks after the funeral, and this song was playing in ear's reach of Dad. It's like Tucker was following him and made sure he was heard at just the right time. A couple of minutes later and the song would have been done.

Please note that the "Ring of Fire" song by Johnny Cash is not a current hit. This was a song from the 1960s. It is unusual that it was heard at all, let alone at such coincidental times (more to come) following Tucker's death.

July 2, 2018, 7:50 a.m.—I went out to move my truck back into the driveway to load up Tucker's thank-you cards. "Broken Halos" came on the radio. We drove up to Pine Lake located north of Merrill to go fishing. A truck advertising skydiving was parked in the parking lot. A bird swooped down into the water and got a fish. To me, this was Tucker's way to show he was skydiving. It was number 2 on his bucket list of things to do before he died. He was fulfilling dreams he could not fulfill here while on earth.

July 8, 2018—A number of buses traveled down to attend a Milwaukee Brewers game to watch the Athens High School state championship baseball team being honored before the game. The team and coaches were lined up in front of the first baseline area before the game. Each had their names announced with their faces magnified on the big screen. A memorable moment for each that will last a lifetime. I made my way down to the front of the stands to take photos. Afterward, I walked over to an area and watched the game so I could be in the sun versus sitting underneath the canopy overhang in the shade where our seats were. A lady stood by me, and we started some small talk. She saw the Athens Bluejay shirt I was wearing and congratulated Athens on their championship. She asked if my son just graduated from the team. I told her that my son was the one who died in the accident just a week and a half before the championship game. She started to cry. She went on to tell me she lost her fourteen-year-old son to cancer. One day she was yelling at him to clean up his room; the next day he was sick and died. It was very sudden. His name was Major, and he enjoyed listening to and playing music. She asked me what Tucker liked for music. I told her about the "Ring of Fire" song he would sing while growing up. She started to cry again. She went on to explain that Major would also sing and play that song. He was playing that song with Tucker in heaven; she was sure of it. Over 160,000 people at the game and this one lady and I met and had this story to share.

July 14, 2018—I was having a conversation with my sister Wanda about how the family was doing. Wanda lives in the mountains of Colorado. It was early in the morning. She was thinking how Tucker would be getting up to get a workout on the weights in and saw a yellow butterfly fly by her, then disappeared. She had to share this as it was like a connection moment that Tucker knew we were talking, and he made his presence known to my sister.

July 15, 2018—Visiting with Dad and Mom. Dad was picking rocks in a field. He told me how nearby a bald eagle seemed to be watching over him from atop a tree. This was near the same field Tucker was supposed to pick rocks on the day of the accident.

July 17, 2018—Wanda was telling a friend about Tucker's loss and was sharing the story about the song "Ring of Fire." Shortly after the friend left, Wanda received a screenshot taken from the friend's car radio. The song that came on as she was traveling home after hearing Wanda's story was "Ring of Fire."

July 17, 2018—Dale was at Tucker's favorite bow stand, preparing for hunting season. About thirty yards from the bow stand was a bald eagle sitting at the top of a tree, watching his every move.

July 19, 2018—A friend of Tucker's was involved in a really bad rollover accident. The vehicle was completely totaled. All the panels were damaged *except* for the glass on the left side rear door where Tucker's T12 sticker was applied. See the photos attached. His friend survived.

July 24, 2018—It's Grandpa Westfall's birthday. Tanner drove Dale and I to their home just before 6:00 p.m. to celebrate for the evening. Tanner didn't like the song on the radio so switched stations. Moments later, the station he switched to played "Broken Halos." There was an eerie (but good) silence in the vehicle as we listened to the song play.

July 29, 2018, 6:30 a.m.—The first dream with Tucker in it that I recall. There were football players in the background. One of Tucker's best friends and he were talking to the football coach. Tucker's right shoulder was slumped forward. He looked at me and said, "Mom, I'm not going to be able to play today." Tucker had dislocated his right shoulder in the accident.

At 9:00 a.m., I watched the movie *Heaven Is for Real* based on a best-selling true story book. It is about a three-year-old boy who has his appendix burst and goes in for emergency surgery. Having a near-death experience, he shares seeing Jesus, angels singing, meeting his dad's grandfather and his little sister that his mom had lost during her pregnancy. The boy describes how beautiful it is during his visit to heaven.

August 3, 2018—I went to the bank to handle a number of transactions and was probably in there for no more than ten to fifteen minutes. During the last transaction to close out Tucker's savings account, "Broken Halos" came on the intercom stereo system in the bank.

August 26, 2018, Sunday, 1:00 a.m.—I could not sleep that night, so I went upstairs to Tucker's room to lie down on his bed. Something told me to lean up and look outside, so I propped myself up. The light across the street was shining through the tree in front of Tucker's room. Rays of light beams were going in all directions. It wasn't like this on a normal occasion. It was so much more beautiful in detail that I can't really put it into words. I just sat and stared at it for several minutes. I lay back down, and after about fifteen minutes, I looked up once again to see it, but it was no longer there.

At 8:35 a.m. (*about the same time Tucker passed away*), I heard rustling on the balcony and looked out my office window. There were five blue jays flying past my window and landed in the large pines in my backyard. A single blue jay came back and landed on the roof by the balcony, so I quickly ran to the bathroom, which overlooks the balcony to get a better look at him. It was as if he was looking back at me as I looked at him through the window. After a few moments, he flew away. Tucker let me know he was with friends and was okay.

August 2018—One of Tucker's best friends had gone on his family's fishing trip in Canada in August. His mom recounted the following story for me. They were taking the boat out onto the water. This friend of Tuck's was in a somber mood. It was overcast and cloudy and looked like it was about to rain. Mom told his son they were making this trip all about Tucker. She said the clouds parted in front of them, the sun shone through, and an eagle flew toward them. They were stunned and looked on in disbelief—but then again—not. She couldn't wait to share this story.

September 14, 2018, 3:25 a.m.—It was very early in the morning. I got up and went to the bathroom. As I was returning to bed, I glanced at the TV receiver to see what time it was. I stopped in my tracks. "Did I just see that?" I had to take a second longer look this time. The letters H-U-N-T were on the receiver display. I woke Dale and asked if he had watched TV downstairs last night (thinking he had messed up the controls somehow), and he said, "No." I stared with excitement at the receiver to make sure of what I was seeing. It must have been another five seconds more and I went to grab my camera but didn't have time to take a photo. The clock display turned back to a regular time, now showing 3:31 a.m. For months since Tucker's death, I had been getting awakened about 3:30 a.m. All I could think was Tucker was trying to send a message to go hunt for him during the upcoming deer season since he was no longer able to. There was no way I was going to let him down. I was going hunting for him.

September 15, 2018—Beef Fest in Edgar was being held at a local farm. Upon entering the fest grounds, we could hear a live band playing under a tent. After walking around for a short time, the band started to play "Country Roads" by John Denver, the same song that began Tucker's funeral.

September 28, 2018—I was making a pumpkin pie in our kitchen. *Hunt* showed up on the TV receiver in the kitchen. This time, I grabbed my cell phone and was able to capture a photo of it before it changed.

September 29, 2018—It was time to hunt for Tucker, so I got myself ready to go sit in a hunting blind. I started putting on Tucker's hunting clothes, pulling them out of his Scentlok case located in the back room. That case was used so the clothes don't pick up household scents that the deer can smell. Suddenly, a blue jay flew down and landed at the base of the steps located just outside this room with a wall of windows. He jumped to the lilac tree located next to the steps and appeared to be watching me. After about thirty seconds, the blue jay flew off. I headed to the kitchen where *Hunt* comes on the TV receiver once more.

October 12, 2018—After spending a few hours in the hunting blind, I returned home folding up Tuck's clothes and carefully placed them back into the Scentlok storage container. It was cold outside, so I decided to put on my pink camouflage bibs and jacket, then pulled Tuck's number 22 football jersey over the top before heading up to Athens High School to watch the Friday night football game. It was important to Tuck not to miss a game—he wanted to be there with the team, and I was the one who would represent him no matter how cold it was outside. What a surprise when I arrived to see the Athens football players were also dressed in pink socks and undergarments. It was the game promoting cancer awareness. I had no idea they would be wearing pink! Another remarkable coincidence?

October 20, 2018, 6:00 p.m.—After sitting in a hunting blind for nearly four weeks, having no luck with seeing deer, I decided to try to sit on my swivel chair in the open woods behind a water hole somewhat hidden behind a tree. Additional cover with branches were gathered and placed in front of me to provide further cover. Having a set of antlers with me, I rattled the horns and waited with anticipation for a deer to respond. Rattling horns will often bring other deer in the area to come and check out what deer are in their territory. It worked. A six-pointer came from the east and headed south up the trail. He stopped and smelled, then turned to walk toward my direction until he smelled my footprints in the snow. At that time, he looked up, facing me square on. I already had the crossbow hairs on him and took a shot. It was a tight shot between branches, but it was a good shot, as he did not run far. I harvested my first buck on my own land just down from Tucker's stand. And I did it with no blind, just sitting on a chair in the open woods. Was Tuck watching this? I'm convinced he was right there with me.

November 1, 2018—Dale's dad shot an eight-pointer near Tucker's stand on my land.

November 2, 2018—This morning was five months to the day post-accident. Dale had his radio alarm come on at 6:02 a.m. The first words spoken when the announcer came on are "I'm very sorry for your loss." She was really referring to losing a basketball game that night *(I think the Celtics)* and was speaking with her copartner on the radio. We, of course, took it differently. The timing of that comment was just unbelievable and a tearjerker.

November 3, 2018—I headed to the cabin to hunt; "Country Roads" played on the radio.

November 14, 2018, 11:21 a.m.—While assisting an American Fence employee at the baseball field inserting black slats into fencing, a large bald eagle flew toward me. The sky was cloudless. I got excited and said, "Did you see the bald eagle? Do you see it?" He walked down to me wondering why I was so excited. We took a break so I could tell him my story and why the bald eagle meant so much.

Country Music Awards was on television tonight. Chris Stapleton won song of the year for "Broken Halos." In his acceptance speech, he told the audience his inspiration in writing this song was for all those who have left us too soon.

November 15, 2018—Tanner shot a doe near Tucker's stand on my land. Looks like the entire family will be successful with harvesting deer this season.

November 29, 2018—Coach Westfall allowed me to meet with the wrestling team at the high school so I could share a Tucker story with them as a form of incentive for the wrestlers to perform well this year. The story started out by showing them a pencil drawing I did of Tucker ten years ago, which depicted how I imagined him to look in the year 2018. Tucker had written at the top, "Tucker in ten years." He was bulked out in neck, shoulder, and leg muscles wearing a singlet. I began by telling the wrestlers that Tuck was not pleased with his freshman performance on the mat last year, so I had placed a sticky on this drawing and placed it on his bed. After I knew he had been in his room and read it, I knocked on his door, went in, and sat down next to him as he was lying in his normal spot on the pillow at the head of his bed. We talked about strengths, weaknesses, and goals. Shortly after, he had started his hand crunches while watching TV, lifting weights, and doing sit-ups and push-ups in his room. He had asked me to take him up to the weight room that opened at 6:00 a.m. every morning. After about a month and a half, the athletic director offered to pick him up because Tuck was continuing on this weight lifting regimen. It worked out well because the athletic director needed to be up there anyway to open up the weight room. His son was often with him, so he and Tucker worked out together. Tucker's goal was to be sitting in a chair in front of the student body for the pep rally for those wrestlers who made it to state. I thanked the wrestlers for letting me share his story, knowing what Tucker wanted to achieve and how he was working toward that goal. I had hoped each wrestler was inspired to work as hard. Coach Westfall then handed out the new wrestling uniforms purchased with funds received from Tucker's funeral. We talked about the #Westfallstrong note taped to each bag and how those words "were Tuck" and meant so much to him. (Connor Westfall later would mention this meeting in a newspaper article after he made it to state wrestling held in February 2019.)

December 1, 2018—We were at the Antigo wrestling tourney, and Tucker's friends wanted to share their own stories about Tucker. Kaden reported his math grades had improved. He thought Tucker was watching over him since Tucker was good at math and science and had always helped him before. Connor's twelve-point buck he got was part Tucker's doing according to his story. His mom saw a cardinal right before hearing about Connor's buck. Marshall got a tattoo on his forearm *(Matthews 5:4—wings TWW 6/2/18)*. Patrick had his class ring engraved with Tucker's name inside the band. Parents and wrestlers gave compliments on the new uniforms. More tears that day, but it was great to hear all the heartfelt stories.

HERE FOR A GOOD TIME, NOT A LONG TIME

December 22, 2018—Relatives on Dale's side stopped by and presented handmade ornaments of Tucker. They shared a story about Uncle Joe, age ninety, who was dying, and did pass away on June 17, just a few weeks after Tucker's accident. Joe was unaware of what had happened with Tucker but said in conversation, "that boy *(didn't refer to him as Tucker)* riding the UTV—he hit a mailbox." No one had told Joe about the details of the accident.

January 18, 2019, 6:40 a.m.—I woke up to "Broken Halos" playing on the radio. Always thinking of Tucker. Grieving.

January 30, 2019, morning—I had another dream with Tucker in it. Do I miss him so much that my nights are sleepless because of my dreams?

January 31, 2019—I was driving home from work appointments in Wausau. "Broken Halos" came on just after I told Tucker I missed him so much. This is a daily struggle to get through the day.

February 9, 2019—I was up at 6:15 a.m. It was wrestling regionals today. Dale was upstairs showering as I got up. My mornings typically begin by winding the two antique clocks in the living room and one in the laundry room. Because they do not keep time accurately, the time needs to be set manually by moving the hands. So this morning, I wound the two clocks in the living room and walked into the laundry room and wound that one. Each clock's hand was manually moved to 6:00 a.m. and chimed six times. Then the hand was moved to 6:15 a.m. I picked up the folded clothes off the dryer that I did last night and walked with my arms full to the bedroom, laying the clothes on the bed to begin putting them away in their respective drawers. The antique clock in the bedroom, which I had not wound since before Tucker's death, chimed six times. I was still standing next to the bed and had not touched the dresser nor that clock. Startled, I turned and stared at the clock while it finished chiming, then smiled and simultaneously broke down into tears, saying, "Tucker." I proceeded to tell him I knew he was here and that I knew he knew what day it was. Regionals meant a lot to him. This was what he had started his weightlifting program for as he had his sights on getting past regionals. Now it's here, and he was not able to compete and beat his competition. We will never know what could have been. This is so sad that his goal will never be realized. I went on to thank him for the sign and told him I knew he'd be with me for the day. Dale came downstairs from taking a shower and saw me crying on the bed. I shared the story of what had just occurred. He turned and walked away in silence.

At 9:44 a.m., we left for regionals being held in Edgar. "Broken Halos" came on the radio.

February 14, 2019—It was Valentine's Day morning. Last night I told Tuck I wish I could feel him, hug him, see him, and that he could talk to me. I felt something on my arm while sleeping—like two fingers pressing on my upper arm. I said, "If this is you, Tuck, thanks, I can feel you. Love you. Miss you."

March 4, 2019—I traveled to Chippewa Falls to inspect damage due to the weight of ice and snow on several greenhouses. Tucker's on my mind. A large bald eagle flew overhead while I was conducting the inspection. The owner of the greenhouses also mentioned noticing the eagle. I told him the bald eagle was watching out for me and that this happens quite a bit.

March 10, 2019—While showering this morning, I left the bathroom door open. The "Happy Birthday" balloon that had been in the living room floated into the bathroom. It stuck up against the interior of the shower wall. I just laughed out loud and said, "Tucker!"

March 27, 2019—Had a meeting in Appleton for work. Tucker's recording was shared with the group and was received well. My manager's neighbor, Lyne V. Reider, is a life coach and inspirational speaker after losing her husband, sisters, and parents. He gave me her book, *Lost & Found: Finding Life After Death* to read. When I left to travel back to the office, I wasn't even five minutes out of Appleton when a bald eagle flew right past my vehicle. It seemed Tucker was aware of where I was, was watching over me, and knew what was being shared with others with approval. That's how I saw it. I hadn't had so many bald eagles so close to me ever.

New Berlin, Wisconsin lottery ticket winner of $768 million—number 12 was the powerball. Number 12 was the number of Tucker's baseball jersey.

April 3, 2019—"Broken Halos" began on the car radio at 12:04 p.m. I had just gotten in the vehicle. I'm thinking it's about the timing, the coincidence. A minute or two later and the song is partially sung or completely over.

April 11, 2019—Snowstorm, rain, and sleet today. School was cancelled. Everyone was home. You know how if one hits their head he/she may see stars. Well, twice this morning, I was sitting at my desk conducting computer work. This single white speck went across in front of me and disappeared. Not sure if there was a speck in my eye or whether it had any meaning, but maybe this was Tucker's way of showing me he was home today too!

April 21, 2019—Easter Sunday early morning dream—Tucker appeared smiling in a flannel plaid shirt. Happy Easter, my sweet son! A blue jay flew in front of my vehicle as our family traveled to Easter dinner that I thought was at our parents' home. When we showed up, no one was there, realizing then that dinner was at Lorene and Tom's home. This means traveling down Silver Leaf Road, passing by the farmhouse where Tucker's accident happened. I could have taken the highway, but for whatever reason, I needed to take this road. As we approached the Amish farmhouse, there was silence in the vehicle as tears began to travel down my cheeks. I didn't want Dale and Tanner to notice, but I think Dale knew I was reliving the moment on Easter Sunday of all days. This day meant a lot to Tucker given his faith, so maybe that's why I took this road. I found myself trying to reason and make sense of things. At the same exact time we were passing this spot, Lorene called on the cell phone inquiring where we were. Talk about timing. Need I say more?

May 1, 2019—I had a meeting in Oshkosh and picked up the Japanese dwarf red maple tree for the sophomore class to plant on behalf of Tucker. "Country Roads" played on the radio while traveling home.

May 3, 2019—Had a dream with Tucker laughing. We were traveling to the state baseball tournament in Appleton on an all-terrain vehicle with our new dog, Spunk. Was Tucker sending another message?

I took off work today since it was the morning of the Tucker Westfall Memorial baseball field dedication. The dedication is expanded on in a separate chapter. Of significance this day is something else that happened with the girls' softball team. Siarra Zinkowich (just happens to wear number 12 on her jersey) hit a home run, had five RBIs, and numerous fly ball catches for outs. It was a spectacular game for her. Siarra was on the hunting crew with Tucker and hasn't hunted with them since his passing. Isn't it most interesting that both Bluejays sporting the same number on their jerseys had such a memorable day?

May 28, 2019—Subregional game against Wausau Newman today. Athens won 8–1. Can't help but wonder if Athens will make another run for state.

May 29, 2019—The Athens baseball team won their regional finals game against Edgar 15–7. Seth Coker hit the first Athens home run at Tucker Westfall Memorial ballpark. How special, given he had been honored with the Tucker Westfall Memorial Scholarship as a graduating senior this year. Athens advances to sectionals to be held next Tuesday in Crivitz. State bound in our sights again!

May 30, 2019—It took four hours to get a Tucker rose tattoo with his name scrolled below it on my left shoulder. I shared my story with the tattoo artist who was grateful he was selected to do this special one which held such meaning in my heart. On the way home, "Broken Halos" played on the radio.

June 2, 2019—It is the one-year anniversary of Tuck's accident. I relive that day from a year ago minute by minute. This morning, in his honor, at 7:00 a.m., I started fire in the firepit. At 8:38 a.m. (pretty close to the time Tucker died), a blue jay flew around the pines by me. At 2:30–3:00 p.m., my sisters, Georgine and Lorene, stopped by for a visit, knowing how difficult today is for our family. While visiting in the backyard, a blue jay was flying from tree to tree. I told them to come down to the fire, which I had stoked up periodically throughout the day. See, I said, "Tucker's here—he wants you to know that he sees you."

At 6:00 p.m., approximately thirty friends and parents stopped by, walking over from Corey Westfall's home. Corey is Tucker's godfather. I had them all take a seat around the firepit and told them the story of the blue jay appearing at select times throughout the day. I was presented with a hand-painted blue jay stone, which read "Bluejays Appear When Angels Are Near." One, especially me, couldn't help but cry as this was so fitting, so absolutely perfect, with today's happenings. Other trinkets and cards were shared, along with a whole lot of hugs. The special tattoo was shown to them.

At 8:00 p.m., Tanner came down to the firepit, which was still burning. A blue jay appeared in the background, flying between pines. We sat and let the fire burn out for the day. A beautiful day to remember a special son and brother.

June 3, 2019—I had a conversation with Dad and Tanner about what I wanted for my upcoming birthday on June 12. The best gift I could ask for would be sitting at the state baseball tournament in Appleton, watching our team play, remembering the dream I had with Tuck and I driving to the game.

June 4, 2019—The Athens baseball team headed to sectionals held in Gilbraltar, Wisconsin. Could they pull out another couple of wins to get to state? Would my dream with Tucker come true? Athens won the first semifinal game 6–4 against Greenwood. After two runs scored, they played "Ring of Fire" between innings. Not planned again—it just happened! Connor Westfall came over by me before the start of the final sectional game where the winner would head to state. I told him I had something to tell him, but there wasn't time because the game was about to start. Athens was down in the score, and it was not looking favorable for us. All of a sudden, I happened to look up at the sky and saw the clouds separate, the sun shone bright, and the other team made some rather simple errors to lose their lead and allow Athens to pull ahead to win the game. Athens ended up defeating Gilbraltar 5–3. It was such an exciting ending. Both of today's games were come-from-behind wins. Athens is headed to state again! As I walked back to my vehicle to take the drive back home, I reflected on that dream the morning of the baseball dedication ceremony, my one birthday wish, and how it had all come true. Smiling, I wondered once again if I had seen the future. I have a secret and want to share it with the team.

June 6, 2019—A mother made a special phone call to tell me her son was working with his dad today and they heard, "Ring of Fire" on the speaker radio system. This mother's son was one of Tucker's close friends and being it was one year to the day from Tuck's funeral, he was so excited since he hadn't heard that song since last year. They both knew the special significance of this day and wanted to share this experience.

June 7, 2019—Tanner and I drove to White Lake to go fishing. At 8:22 a.m., Tanner switched the radio channel. The song finished, and one would not believe it, but "Ring of Fire" began to play.

June 11, 2019—There was a send-off parade for the Athens baseball team headed to the state. I asked if I could speak to the team on the bus before it took off to Appleton. The players boarded the bus and took their seats. The pastor, the coaches, and I followed behind. The talking stopped, and all became silent except for the bus motor. I started to speak. However, I have a soft-toned voice, so the bus driver shut the engine down while I spoke. I went on to tell the group how I had wanted to share a dream I had with Coach Westfall, but he wasn't interested in hearing it. I asked Coach Coker if he recalled when we were on the ball field talking and how I wanted to share a story with him but that Coach Westfall thought I was crazy, so I was holding off. Then I turned to Connor Westfall and spoke directly to him, asking if he remembered before the sectionals final game when he approached me to talk and that I wanted to tell him something, but there wasn't time. He nodded, acknowledging that he remembered. Well, now was the time, and I was able to share it with the whole team, not caring what they or anyone thought of me. This dream involved Tucker, those were his friends and teammates, and they needed to hear about this. So I went on telling them about this dream I had on the morning of May 3, 2019, baseball field dedication where Tucker and I were driving to the state stadium in a UTV. We both knew this team was going to state and I was bursting to share my dream and what I knew. I told them I didn't know how it was going to happen, just that it was going to happen. Then I explained in April I had checked the schedule and saw the state tournament fell on my birthday and how I talked to Tucker and told him the best birthday wish I could ask for would be sitting at the state tourney in the front row, watching the team play. I was taken aback a bit on how this wish had actually come true.

No one was home that night. Tanner went fishing in South Dakota. Coach Westfall had traveled down on the bus with the team, so I slept (barely) in Tucker's room, waiting for the hours to pass by with anticipation of the sun rising so I could be at the state tourney sitting in that very front row.

June 12, 2019—Travel to state, leaving at 5:00 a.m. for an 8:00 a.m. start time. The team was scheduled to play against a very tough Webster team. Dale's dad accompanied me. At the end of the third inning, "Ring of Fire" played. Once again I was in disbelief at the coincidence of this song playing of all songs during our game. Just another sign that Tucker was with us. Athens ended up losing the close semifinal game to Webster 4–3. Although Athens did not advance further, I couldn't help but reflect on the dream, the wish, and that Tucker knew. I knew.

June 23, 2019—Our family left on a fishing vacation to Michigan—Traverse City and Lake St. Clair with Lorene and Tom.

June 27, 2019—Tanner, Dale, and Tom fished Lake St. Clair for walleye and smallmouth bass. Tucker's missing in the photos. It was hard. This was not the same. He should be there.

June 28, 2019—As part of our vacation, we visited Fredrick Gardens in Grand Rapids. Because our dog, Spunk, was with us, I was not allowed in, so I sat on a bench outside. A mother and three kids came up to me while I was sitting. I could see the mother was holding something in her hand, so I asked what it was. She opened her hand, and there in her palm was a gold pin of a bald eagle, which she told me that she had stepped on, and it went into her flip-flop sandal. I couldn't help but think this was another message that Tuck wanted me to know he was on this trip with us. He was near.

June 29, 2019—We were traveling back home from vacation and just past Stevens Point, Tanner switched the radio station. "Broken Halos" came on. We noticed a couple bald eagles flying overhead when we neared Kronenwetter a short distance later. Tuck knew we were coming home.

July 23, 2019—This day I traveled to a client's residence to check out a wind claim. A very large bald eagle landed on a tree above me while I was conducting the inspection. I shared Tucker's story with the homeowner. He teared up having his own story to share. He believes in the signs I have been seeing and what I was telling him. Their town suffered a similar tragedy of a seventeen-year-old football player, Owen Knutson, who died flying in his plane in 2017. He explained their community had a beautiful memorial service at the school for him. A little boy with autism saw a crane flying by at one of the gatherings for the Knutson family. The boy said it was a boy who died flying through to see everyone. The little boy knew nothing about the incident.

July 30, 2019—Dad went to check on Tucker's tree stand. The tree had fallen over due to very strong winds and found the tree damaged but no damage to the tree stand itself. As I mentioned early on in this book, Tucker was always very protective of his belongings. I think he was looking out for his tree stand.

August 4, 2019, morning—Two dreams today. Tucker sitting in a chair at party. Two older friends were in that dream. In a second dream, Tucker was wearing his number 22 football jersey, and I was talking to him.

At 12:30 p.m., Dale and I stopped at his aunt and uncle's home. Those same two friends in my dream were sitting in the garage, having a drink with others. My mind immediately went to the dream. Was I once again seeing the future? Not sure what to make of this. I shared this story with Dale. With regard to the second dream, football practice begins tomorrow, August 5, 2019.

August 8, 2019—Football practice was scheduled two times a day to get the players prepared for the season. This morning, Dale came back from practice and reported that a bald eagle was flying overhead across the road where practice was being held.

August 10, 2019—Dale said the bald eagle was flying across the road again at football practice. Tucker knew what time of the year it was!

August 19, 2019—I attended an insurance class in Green Bay. Each person in the class took turns introducing themselves and spoke about their families. I wasn't ready to talk about my family, and I was getting more and more nervous as the introductions went around the tables, and then it was my turn. It was too much too soon. I started by telling them about Dale and my son, Tanner, then broke down crying and through tears shared our loss of Tuck. The instructor thought it was best to take a break. One of the elderly students approached me, giving me a hug and sharing his own story of his seventeen-year-old daughter who had died and how there were signs afterward like lights flickering on and the TV turning on suddenly. I told him: Don't ignore the signs. They (who pass) want you to know they are okay and look for ways to show you. I'm certain of it.

August 22, 2019—Traveled to Cincinnati for our August company meeting.

August 24, 2019—After the Saturday morning meetings were concluded at approximately 11:30 a.m., I had time left before my 6:00 p.m. flight, so I walked to Cincinnati's central park area. A large water fountain was bubbling, music was blaring over the intercom, and I immediately noticed a large digital billboard displaying different ads. The main ad was "Ring of Fire: The Music of Johnny Cash" which was currently playing at a theater in Cincinnati. Another one of those I-can't-believe-it moments, but there it was. I took a photo on my cell phone and sent it to my sisters. Shortly after seeing the billboard, "Ring of Fire" came on over the intercom system and played. It was just incredibly special having this feeling once again that Tucker was watching over me.

August 25, 2019—I met with a friend regarding a home and land she had for sale following the passing of her mother and father as she no longer resided in this area. With tears and happy thoughts, she shared signs of her parents, and I told her about the many signs I had received, the psychic medium, the baseball field done for Tucker, and other happenings that were unexplained. She encouraged me to write a book.

September 18, 2019—It's *Wednesday* night, and remember, Tucker said he never missed Wednesday nights. I was flipping through the television channels and country music came on from 7:00–9:00 p.m. It caught my eye because it was about the start of country music featuring Johnny Cash and Elvis Presley. Something told me to leave it on this channel and watch. Near the end of the show, "Ring of Fire" played. Of course, I was thinking Tucker knew this was coming, and he wanted me to watch. There seems to be this sense or feeling, and when I follow it, I usually understand why, as there is some special meaning behind it. The history of country music, discussions with Roseanne Cash, and how Johnny Cash wrote "I Walk the Line," intended to say he would not stray from his wife. But then he enjoyed his fame and met June Carter. She wrote "Ring of Fire" to express the experience of falling in love with the married man in black, knowing he was no longer staying loyal to his wife.

September 27, 2019—It was Friday night football at Greenwood. I talked to Tuck throughout the game. At one point, I told him it sure would be nice to see Greenwood fumble. They fumbled and recovered the ball. Well, I told him that didn't work, but can it happen again? Sure enough, a second fumble the following play, and Athens recovered. No way. Is Tuck making this happen? Later in the fourth quarter, I said it sure would be nice if Athens caught a pass about now. The quarterback had not passed much the entire game. Well, once again, one wouldn't believe it, but the Athens QB threw up a pass, and the Athens receiver caught the football for a huge gain to set up for a score near the goal line. Four tries later, Athens got into the end zone for a score. Athens won 12–6.

There was a strong sense of Tucker's presence. I so badly want to run out and give his teammates high fives and chest bumps (well, maybe not chest bumps), to join in the celebration. I know how much that would have meant to Tuck to be a part of that win. In a way, maybe he was!

September 28, 2019—Attended the cross-country meet in Oshkosh where Tanner was a participant. A bald eagle was flying over the golf course on the course where they ran.

October 8, 2019—When Dale and I returned home tonight from watching Tanner's cross-country meet in Auburndale, we went to the kitchen to get food. Spunk, our dog, stood in the entryway leading to the living room, barking at something. Oddly, he walked quickly across the living room rug as if he was following someone and sat at the base of the steps that takes you upstairs. He stood there looking up the steps. My thoughts on this. Is that Tucker? Did he know that Tanner had just medaled (*taking fourteenth place*) with the team placing second at this meet, and Tucker was going be there to congratulate his brother? I can't help but wonder and wish I had a way to get confirmation. All I can do is note these experiences.

November 8, 2019—I traveled to Eau Claire today. As I returned, traveling between Stanley and Thorp, I asked Tuck if he was happy and to show me a sign, and a bald eagle flew over my vehicle. When I returned home and parked in the garage, "Broken Halos" came on the radio. If that doesn't tell you something, not sure what does.

November 16, 2019—Went out to eat at a local restaurant with Lorene and Tom to celebrate Tanner's conference cross-country win. Dale and I had also received the Distinguished Service Award for service to athletics. When we left at 8:08 p.m., we got in the vehicle and "Ring of Fire" came on the radio. Tucker did not want to be left out of the celebration and wanted us to know he was sharing in this special evening of celebration as well!

November 23, 2019—Dad shot a thirteen-pointer on the opening drive first day of deer hunting. I was thinking Tuck had a hand in making this a very special birthday present to Dad. So many good things were happening to our family over the past year and a half.

November 27, 2019—Spunk was sitting on the rug in the dining room. He sat up and looked toward the living room with a very intent look and started barking like something or someone was there, but no one was home, but me. I told Spunk that Tuck likes to visit.

December 14, 2019—Went to the Wabeno wrestling tourney today where the team took third place. Following Carter Brunke's first match, when the ref raised Carter's hand to announce the win, I swear I saw a silver star flash come over his head and went straight up in the air. I said, "Tucker." I knew he was there watching. Carter was the only one to take first place today.

January 11, 2020—Travel to New Richmond for wrestling tourney. A blue jay flew across into my lane during my travels. Tucker knew where I was headed. I attempted to change lanes near Menomonie, Wisconsin, on I-94, and my 2018 Ford Explorer seized up suddenly, and I could not go. The Service Advance Trac warning light came on. Just barely was I able to move back over to the right lane and got off the first exit to a Kwik Trip. This was not a good sign, as when I shifted into park, the transmission jerked. Then I tried placing the transmission in reverse, and it jerked wildly. Trying to accelerate brought little speed. I needed to search for the nearest Ford dealership, or I would be missing the tournament today, and I was not happy about that possibility. Just my luck, there was a Ford service center just five miles down the road off the next exit. Hoping I could get there, I started out driving. It was slow. "Broken Halos" started playing on the radio. Somehow I knew everything would be all right. Tucker was with me, and he was going to take care of me. I was able to drive slowly and made the five miles to the dealership. The service center was not open, but within fifteen minutes, the sales rep had placed me in a Ford Fusion, and I was on my way. I missed a few of the first matches but, for the most part, was able to watch the wrestling team. Pretty darn special. Tucker knew I didn't want to miss the tournament and he found ways to protect and keep me safe. It was a very comforting feeling.

January 16, 2020—Dale ordered wrestling shirts and pants through Rudis for the team. After separating out everyone's order, there was one pair of small-sized sweatpants leftover. Can't help but think Tuck knew I would have wanted a pair and made it happen. Dale actually said the same thing as he threw the pants at me.

January 25, 2020—Athens youth wrestling tourney. The first little boy who showed up to register and check in was named Tucker. What are the odds?

February 1, 2020—Marawood Conference wrestling tournament at Chequamegon (Park Falls). I spoke with Dan Engel about his cabin and fishing at Tucker Lake. How cool? Even a lake named after him! Even more meaningful is the Engels, who have become very special in our lives, fish there.

Unfortunately, an emotional day took place in Athens as this was the day Dale's friend and my classmate's funeral was taking place after losing a yearlong fight with cancer. We were at the wrestling tourney, so we missed the funeral. However, pictures were sent to us, showing fire truck ladders raised on each side of the village. The ladders were joined by the American flag flying in between. A very honorable way to be remembered. Lorene and Tom attended and said that upon leaving the village following the visitation, "Ring of Fire" played on the radio. Thoughts of lost loved ones in the air!

February 2, 2020—A historic Super Bowl was taking place as it was the one hundredth year. San Francisco 49ers versus Kansas City had the honor of playing. KC won 30–20. While watching the game, Dale asked me to look at a photo he had taken a few months ago when visiting the gravestone at the cemetery. He pointed to a maple leaf on the stone right next to Tucker's name. Tucker liked maple trees, sat in maple trees, and a maple tree was planted for him at the high school. Just another sign that can't be ignored.

February 26, 2020—I was working at my work computer. A white spec crossed in front of me like it had before. A feeling of Tucker being present came over me, and I called out to him. It was very special that he stayed near.

March 9, 2020—"Broken Halos" came on the radio as I was traveling to Eau Claire to attend a mediation. This song had come on at various times in my travels over the past weeks. Always thinking of you, Tuck!

School and worldwide shutdown due to COVID-19

March 16, 2020—I traveled to Cameron High School for an appointment. Not being familiar with the area, I drove in and wondered where to park. I had parked and then decided to move and turn my vehicle, then thought I should move ahead a little further. I did this and placed my vehicle in park, still not quite knowing if I parked in the right spot. I looked to my left. There was a sign that read: *"Perhaps they are not the stars, but rather openings in heaven where the love of our lost ones pours through and shines down upon us to let us know they are happy."* This brought tears to my eyes. I guess I parked in the perfect spot. That was a sign of signs…literally.

March 21, 2020—First day of vacation. "Broken Halos" came on just as I was backing out of the driveway. I headed to pick up three Amish boys to help me load debris into dumpsters at the Stevens Point home that we were rehabbing for Tanner to use while he attends college there. One of the Amish boys, named Benjamin, just celebrated his fifteenth birthday. He sat in the front with me. I thought that was significant as Tuck was fifteen, and the other two boys, Moses, age thirteen and Amos, age nineteen, both chose to sit in the back seat. I treated them with Domino's Pizza (which they loved), candies, and twenty dollars each. In three hours, the thirty-yard dumpster was filled.

May 11, 2020—My work took me to the Eagle River airport in Wisconsin to meet with an insured. I typically do not venture out this far, as this location loss is outside my territory, but for some reason, I felt a need to go and went to meet with this insured. Upon arriving, I noticed an eagle statue hanging about three-fourths up on the gable side on the outside of the metal hangar. After meeting, I learned he was a member of the Warbirds. He was a kind man and asked about my kids. With hesitation, I told him about Tanner and then halted and got choked up a bit before sharing my story of Tucker and how he passed. He listened intently and once I was finished, he, too, had his own story to share about his daughter who also passed away from cancer. Their family took every effort to help her, even taking her to a cancer center in Houston, Texas. What? I couldn't believe what I was hearing again. This facility is the same center that my cousin, Kristle, flew to with her husband by her side to see if there was any further care that could be done to save her life. This was the reason we met—this was the reason our stories were being shared. This was why I was supposed to make this trip and be here. I was truly touched by this connection. Then he told me his story of being involved in two near-death experiences. The first being when he was in an airplane (age sixty-four) with his buddy at the controls and the second while he was driving a motorcycle (age sixty-nine) in Kansas City and was rear-ended by a semi-tractor trailer attempting to move over for a merging vehicle. I completed my work and thanked him, leaving somewhat dazed by what just happened.

May 16, 2020—Graduation Day for Tanner and happy seventeenth birthday, Tucker. Not sure why these ceremonious days seem to fall on multiple occasions going on, but it has happened again by coincidence or on purpose! A balloon release was planned in our backyard in front of the firepit. Two weeks ago, the weather showed rain in the forecast. About three days out, the weather changed to partly sunny. The day before, the weather indicated sixty-seven degrees and rain to come in the evening. I told Tucker for weeks what was going on and that I needed light winds out of the east. Guess what? The winds were east 9 mph and just perfect for the balloon release.

Both celebrations took place with birthday balloons being placed on Tucker's tree at the high school and graduation balloons placed on the mailbox in front of our house for Tanner. Tanner's track coach stopped in to deliver a special congratulatory message and took Tanner's photo in his cap and gown.

The backyard had to be prepared for the balloon release. Wood stakes were placed six feet apart to conform with the social distancing guidelines (*due to COVID rules*). I purchased a helium balloon tank about a week earlier and when I went to use it about one and a half hours before the release, the nozzle was defective and had let the helium release from the tank. Panic set in! Thinking fast, I took the balloons and strings to Dollar General located down the street to have them blow up seventeen balloons at two dollars each. I got back just before 6:00 p.m. to start tying each balloon to pre-drilled holes in the wood stakes. Made it in time, and the balloons were all set to go by 6:15 p.m. Just in time too because family and friends started to show up. Georgine, Lorene, and Tom showed at 6:00 p.m. Grandma and Grandpa Westfall showed at 6:05 p.m. Fifteen of Tucker's friends began showing up via special invitation about 6:15 p.m. for the 6:30 p.m. release time. Each of the following stood in front of a balloon: Brody Lipinski, Kaden Redmann, Patrick Redmann, Carter Brunke, Dayne Diethlem, Jake Denzine, Trystan Cator, Alex Mengel, Autumn Westfall, Dayna Ellenbecker, Shauna Belter, Cobie Ellenbecker, Kyler Ellenbecker, Connor Westfall, and Tanner Westfall. Corey Westfall and Lorene, godparents, took the other two spots. I sat in front of them on the steps leading to the firepit and read Happy Birthday in Heaven. After that, Tanner went around and cut the ribbons toward the tips of each balloon while each person hung onto the tip of the balloon. The ribbons were cut so that the balloons were free and would not get caught on anything for environmental safety reasons. Tanner counted down the release—three, two, one. Everyone let their balloon lift, watching them gently drift away to the east. I told Tucker to send a message letting me know he was around and saw this. About thirty seconds later, a small propeller plane, red and white, did a flyover. That was not planned by me! I can only hope that he had something to do with it. Just can't make this stuff up! Perfect day for Tucker and Tanner!

June 2, 2020—The firepit was going all day for Tuck again to commemorate the two-year anniversary of his passing. A mom of Tucker's close friend stopped over about 5:00 p.m. A blue jay showed up as we were enjoying the fire and talking about Tuck.

June 27, 2020—A beautiful sunny day in the eighties with just a slight breeze for Tucker's third annual golf outing. There were eighteen teams participating and really nice raffle prizes. Good times had by all. "Ring of Fire" was played on the jukebox.

June 28, 2020—Went to Willow Springs to sell more raffle tickets for a large quilt being raffled off. A few more raffle tickets needed to be sold following the golf outing. "Ring of Fire" was played at 12:48 p.m. at the festival. A number of people stopped at the booth and inquired of Tucker's story and where the proceeds would go. This ordeal is still very difficult to talk about. Enough tickets were sold to pick a raffle winner at the end of the day. Proceeds go toward the football, baseball, and wrestling programs at Athens High School.

July 5, 2020—Dale and I were sitting on the front porch in the evening. A very scarce bird, a cedar waxwing, was by Dad's truck parked in the driveway. He flew from the ground up to the bed of the truck. He jumped in front of Tucker's symbol that was stickered on the back window. He got close and tapped his beak toward it like he's saying, "I know that's me." He flew up to the roof. I took a photo of it. That's Tucker!

August 26, 2020—Traveled to Shawano to meet with my manager. My manager is a very caring individual and wants to know how our family is coping, so the conversation involved Tucker. On my travels back, an eagle flew overhead, flying in the same direction I was headed. Shortly after, two white specks appeared in my vehicle and moved from the steering wheel to the left middle console area. Tuck must be with me, and he knew what was going on.

September 1, 2020—First day of classes for Tucker as a senior.

September 28, 2020—I had a dream with Tucker. Our family stepped into a restaurant. At the bar were two kids sitting on bar stools behind their parents. The male was leaning up against the bar; the female was sitting on a bar stool at the bar. The male was handsome and stood very tall—about seven foot six. The female was pretty with long black hair. I saw the boys immediately, and Tucker was one of them. I walked up to him and said, "Hi, Tucker!" He responded, "My name is not Tucker." I asked him, "What is your name?" He said, "Whouton (or Houton?)" He said his last name, but it was muffled. I turned to the parents and explained what happened to my son Tucker. They were very sad to hear this. But I said, "This is Tucker. He looks like him. He smiles like him. He talks like him (about age three)." I asked Whouton, "When is your birthday? When were you born?" He said May 3, 2018. Ironically, this is the month and day of Tanner's birthday (born in different year). I drifted away from the dream.

I got to see Tucker. It seemed so real. Does he make this happen? I researched the name *Houton* on the website and found this:

> H is for heart, warm and loving
> O is for outgoing, so sociable are you
> U is for useful, always to others
> T is for time, you give to friends
> O is for outlook, pleasing to all.
> N is for nifty, how neat!

October 11, 2020—Dad has been hunting a bear with friends who use dogs to pick up tracks for about the past three weeks, without success. Today was the last day he could go bear hunting, as he would return to school on Monday. One dog, named Tucker, started a track on a bear and got the hunt going. Tucker was pulled to rest while fresh dogs were let go to continue to run the bear until the bear ran up a tree. Dad shot a 137-pound bear and was having the skin tanned.

October 24, 2020—Athens football versus St. Point Pacelli on Saturday.

Athens won 44–35. Two events stood out. Near the end of the second quarter, I said to Tucker it sure would be nice if one of the guys could run one all the way back for a touchdown. Wouldn't you know it, an Athens player broke free from the kickoff and nearly ran the entire length of the field before being tackled just short of the goal line. It was enough to set the team up for a score. Then, during the third quarter, I said to Tucker, it sure would be nice to have Pacelli fumble since they were so close to our end zone. The very next play, Pacelli fumbled. Athens recovered. I just said, "Tucker, how do you do that?" Amazing!

February 3, 2021—The Athens wrestling team would be at sectionals in Saint Croix Falls on Saturday. I was trying to get a pass to go since only two persons were allowed per wrestler *(due to COVID restrictions)*. No coaches could have an extra person attend. I reached out to other local coaches in the conference for extra tickets, but it did not look promising that I could get a ticket. For whatever reason, the push was on (someone over my shoulder maybe), and it was important to be there. This morning when I came upstairs to work, a photo had fallen off the refrigerator and lay on the floor. It was one of my favorite pictures of Tucker in a wrestling move pinning the other guy. I said out loud to Tucker as I was picking up the photo to place it back on the refrigerator, "I know, Tucker. I am trying to get a ticket." So what happened? The athletic director phoned around lunch hour trying to get ahold of me, leaving a message on my cell phone and calling Dale's cell phone, trying to get ahold of one of us to tell us he would receive a ticket to attend as an athletic director and was willing to give the ticket to me so that I could attend. I didn't even know what to think, other than to think this was just another sign!

February 11, 2021—The Athens High School boys' basketball team took first place in the conference after seventy-two years. It was a great game followed by a memorable post-game. After the game, team members cut down the nets with one net lying across the conference trophy and the other pieced up as a keepsake for each player. Tucker's friends and senior players, Dayne Diethelm and Cobie Ellenbecker, approached me each giving me a hug, thanking me for coming to watch. A very special and tearful moment.

April 17, 2021—I had been working on a project for the village and was trying to figure out a way to get a life-size draft horse statue transported back from New Hampshire. Behind the statue was a dray with logs. The display was a representation of how Athens was founded as a logging town. The horse and dray would be a unique greeting display to those who enter our village from the north side of Athens. I told Dale, Tanner, Tom, and Lorene that I was planning to make the trip out to New Hampshire to pick it up by renting an Enterprise flatbed truck. No one wanted me to make the trip out there alone.

April 18, 2021—Dale and I met with Tom at Miltrim Farms to get spliced tires to be used for cushioning on the flatbed trailer for the horse. Dale was washing them off with the power washer, and one of Tom's weekend employees showed up in a vehicle displaying a Vermont license plate. Dale struck up a conversation with the employee. He was headed to Vermont next week. Tom and I approached him about the draft horse in New Hampshire to see if he would pick it up and transport it back to Wisconsin. His response was that next week he'd have a van but that he would be headed out in June with a flatbed trailer and could haul it back. He also would be stopping in Lake Erie to walleye fish—the very same place we had researched to go fishing. This was all too good to be true! I thought Tucker had a lot to do with hearing me and making this happen. The timing, the circumstances, and the situation were all too connected.

April 29, 2021—First baseball game of the year at Tucker Westfall Memorial Field. A bald eagle flew around the ball field. Athens beat Wausau Newman 5–3.

May 2, 2021—Tanner and I were sitting on the porch at 4:45 p.m. talking. "Broken Halos" played on the radio.

May 13, 2021—Met with Grandma Engel, the person who made the stickers of Tucker's "12" and "22" symbols with wings designed by her daughter. I brought her five roses and told her it would be Tucker's eighteenth birthday on Sunday. I then shared the story with her about seeing a psychic medium and how Tucker came forth and was trying to tell the medium about knowing these symbols and numbers were made for him. Tucker knew these stickers symbolized him and how important the Engels were in honoring him. Tears were shared.

May 16, 2021—Tucker's eighteenth birthday. Eighteen roses and balloons were displayed on the dining room table in his memory. Received several text messages from those thinking of us. I was painting the village gazebo today. When I returned home at 9:22 p.m., the front porch was full of happy birthday balloons tied all over the place. I learned later that a bunch of Tucker's friends stopped by and left them. They were a group of some of the most loyal friends anyone could ever ask for. Tucker was very fortunate to have had them in his life. Georgine, Lorene, Wanda, and Autumn put together a message book filled with special memory statements prepared by classmates as a keepsake. Another day of tearful reflection on the impression Tucker made on many. He was so missed.

May 25, 2021—I awoke at 2:08 a.m. with two happy birthday balloons knocking at my head. They startled me a bit as I grabbed the ribbons tickling at my ear, until I saw what time it was and felt that Tucker was near. These were two of the balloons brought over on Tucker's birthday by his friends that had been placed all around the front porch. Many of the balloons still have helium in them and had been floating around in the dining room for the past week. These two balloons traveled from the dining room, across the entryway, into the living room, and made a left into our bedroom, just happening to have floated above the pillow where I was sleeping. Now, in my mind I tried to make sense of it, but it could mean only one thing—Tucker was wishing me a happy birthday, which was coming up in a couple of weeks. He had to make this happen before the helium ran out. It was creative and witty—just like him! I took a couple of photos of the balloons by my pillows on the bed. No one would believe this, but there was no other way to explain the route of the balloons. It was well after 3:00 a.m. when I drifted back asleep. By morning, the balloons had fallen and were near the floor. Once again, I couldn't

HERE FOR A GOOD TIME, NOT A LONG TIME

make this stuff up, but I could share what happened, and one could draw their own conclusions. Tucker's near and dear and showed me in so many ways. That morning I told Dale about the balloons. He tried to tell me about how the air flowed in the home, but when I reminded him that the balloons had been in the dining room for the past week, he shrugged it off. I was in disbelief that he was not accepting of what happened. I felt bad for him and great for me! Then he wondered why nothing happened to him. I reinforced to him that first he needed to believe. Why would Tucker want to work so hard to get his attention if he wasn't willing to believe?

July 1, 2021—I left for Eau Claire for an appointment. As I was traveling, a bald eagle flew overhead. Then, at 8:08 a.m., the radio station 106.5 played "Ring of Fire." As the song played to honor firefighters, my thoughts reflected on memories of my son.

July 10, 2021—Eight blue jays made a lot of noise around Tucker's firepit this morning, so I took a photo of them, thinking Tucker had as many friends here as he does in heaven and wants me to know he is okay.

July 12, 2021—"Broken Halos" came on at 5:05 a.m. this morning while I was watering the village flowers. Guess he was keeping me company!

September 11, 2021—I weed-wacked Tucker Westfall Memorial's ball field fence line. As I was leaving, it was routine for me to give Tucker's bust a loving pat with the palm of my hand on his face. Today, a blue jay was at the start of the school driveway sitting at the top of the tree, squawking away. I stopped and watched him, then waited. He flew toward me, over the bust, and landed at the top of a maple tree located to the south of the ball field. While stooped there, he turned and faced me, squawking a few times as if he was watching me watching him. I shouted out, "I know it's you, Tuck. Thanks for reaching out and watching over me." He flew off, and I walked down the rest of the concrete walkway to my vehicle, leaving with good thoughts.

I shared this story and my dream with Dad later that night. He wished Tucker would do that to him. I told him, "First, you need to believe!"

September 14, 2021—Dad came home from driving a truck at Miltrim all day and shared with me that a bald eagle was on a dead raccoon on the side of the road. I asked him, "Do you believe now?" I told him that Tucker heard us and that was probably why he saw what he did today. He should not ignore his signs. Maybe this was a small turning point for Dad?

September 23, 2021—I was sitting on my land next to the food plot that was set up for deer hunting season. One blue jay came in, then two showed up together. Then there was a ruckus. Seven blue jays showed up, squawking like crazy. I whispered, "Tucker, you brought all your friends over for a visit." The blue jays flew to a nearby acorn tree and started knocking acorns off the tree. I heard acorns falling to the ground and continued watching with amazement. What were they doing? Then they flew just above the tree where I was sitting briefly before flying away. Not even thirty seconds later, I heard movement of leaves rustling in the woods and heard something walking slowly nearby. I perked up with excitement suspecting it was a buck but never saw eyes on it. I really thought Tucker and his friends were trying to have that buck come my way.

September 25, 2021—Aunt Irene (my mom's sister) mailed a letter to me. Upon opening it, she started out by asking if I believe in psychics. Her husband (my uncle Tom) recently died, and the psychic made mention of certain things that pinpointed to her husband. The psychic spoke about loved ones of others who were also in attendance and was spot-on. The psychic came back to Aunt Irene, looked at her, and asked about an ATV or UTV accident that occurred. Aunt Irene responded, stating it occurred three years ago and involved her great nephew. The psychic went on to say that it was just a fluke how the accident happened, but even more, even if that accident hadn't happened, something would have happened soon after because his time on earth was up. The psychic then stopped and looked at Aunt Irene again and said, "He wants you to tell his mom to move on, and he is okay and at peace!" The psychic went on to say that his unusual name will carry on.

Aunt Irene knows about the baseball field being dedicated to him and about the scholarship set up in his name but also thinks babies will be named in his honor.

When I read this and reread it to absorb each written word from my aunt, I took comfort that Tucker sent just one more message, just one more sign, showing how close he was. How powerful that he was able to communicate once again in getting a message to me. It showed how much he cared and wanted me to be comforted. And, yes, I knew all along he was in a good place and at peace; however, for me to move on when every day passes with one of the most precious things in my life gone is the part I struggle with daily. I will move on as I have since the very moment I knew he was gone, but I will always be moving in a different direction and having endless thoughts of what type of togetherness our family should be sharing and can no longer get back. As a mom, I will never recover from this. I cope, and I do so daily with a very broken heart.

TRACY WESTFALL

6/19/2018

Wanda's Friend
7/17/2018

Tucker's Friend's Car
7/19/2018

HERE FOR A GOOD TIME, NOT A LONG TIME

TV Receiver 9/14/2018 & 9/28/2018
9/29/2018

TRACY WESTFALL

Birthday Balloon In Shower
3/10/2019

13-Point Buck Opening Drive
Opening Day Of Hunting
11/23/2019

HERE FOR A GOOD TIME, NOT A LONG TIME

Tucker In Ten Years
11/29/2018

6/2/2019

5/16/2020
Balloon Release Invitation

Cincinnati Billboard
8/24/2019

5/16/2020 Balloon Release

CHAPTER 13

The High School Years/ Scholarship/Senior Year 2021

First, I have to explain some references to the coronavirus disease referred to as COVID-19. The virus that originated from China in December 2019 had been causing havoc across the world and dominated the news and lives of everyone in 2020, 2021, and into 2022. The virus spread quickly from person to person, affecting the lungs with pneumonia-like symptoms that took away breathing capability and overwhelming hospitals across the world with many forced to be on ventilators. It became a pandemic. By the end of 2020, the United States surpassed more than 346,000 deaths, and globally there were more than 1.8 million people who had died. As of January 2022, that number was almost 5.7 million. It caused restricted social gatherings and affected how schools and businesses operated. Stay-at-home orders would be implemented across the country off and on over the course of those years in an effort to slow the spread of the virus as vaccines were developed. Mask mandates were a common theme throughout the world.

*****

August 2020

It would have been the start of Tucker's Senior High School year ending with graduation in May of 2021. This is a milestone year special for anyone, even the parents, looking forward to their child going through their final year of high school.

I struggled with many events that were part of the normal school year. Knowing Tucker would not have missed a football game, I represented him by wearing his 22 jersey while watching the games on the sidelines. After games, I would come home and share with him team highlights while sitting on his bed just like we used to. I felt his presence in the air during the games, but I knew we would have "our time" after the games to talk about plays, touchdowns, misreads, and stuff like that, so if he couldn't talk, I would. Students would not be allowed to have a dance for homecoming following the game due to COVID-19, which was another downer.

The football team, parents, community representatives, and coaches presented Dale and me with a football with Tucker's photo on it and a 24" x 36" framed photo of Tucker with all the seniors' autographs on it. He loved autographed items. He already had autographed items of the Green Bay Packers, the Wisconsin Badgers, Ken Chertow from his Wrestling Camp, and the Athens State baseballs. These were some of his most prized possessions. I know he loved the photo with his buddies' names all over it. It's displayed in my office.

The 2020–2021 wrestling season was really different due to the pandemic. I attended those matches and tournaments that were able to be held. Tucker would have been the only senior on the team that year, but who knows, he may have done some recruiting. After wrestling, baseball season began with his senior classmates. The team did not make it out of regionals that year, and the season ended earlier than it had during those previous baseball championship days.

All this didn't matter. It was really about the senior year and sharing it with his friends, and he wasn't there to do that. For those close friends, the void left by Tucker cannot be filled, and I feel deeply for their hurt and wish I could make it go away for them as they have endured so much. In many ways, I have bonded with his friends in a way most mothers would never have imagined. Most high school kids avoid talking to parents! They instead approached me, exchanged stories of Tucker, and were getting and giving hugs of support both ways. We have cried many a tear together, so when I see them I know they have Tucker in their thoughts. I have shared things that have happened that can only be because of Tucker because I think they should be shared. I think Tucker wants his friends to know he really isn't far away and is watching over us.

Junior Prom, March 2021

Due to the pandemic, the high school canceled what would have been Tucker's junior class prom.

That was very sad as every student looked forward to their high school years, and the prom was just one event where those memories would last forever. I had heard that many girls had already bought their prom dresses and guys had placed down payments on rented tuxes. Although the class had voted, no one knew who was king or queen. Would they ever get to have a prom during their high school years?

Well, you can't go backward, but the parents weren't going to let their kids down. They organized a prom to be held on March 27, 2021, not at the high school, but at the Athens Community Hall. I was not told about it; no parent told me about it. I think Dale and Tanner were trying to protect me. I learned late in the day that prom was going on that evening. It took me by surprise, and I reacted with many tears knowing Tucker wasn't here to take part with his buddies. I knew they were all looking forward to hanging out together, dressing up, going to dinner, and having a good time at the dance. If you recall, Tucker and I had spoken about his prom years before while sitting on his bed. We were both looking forward to this day, and now neither one of us were there. It became a very emotional day for me. I wished my family or some of the parents had prepared me. About 1:00 p.m., two of Tucker's best friends showed up at my door with their girlfriends accompanying them. I saw them through the windows as I went to the door and greeted them, crying. One of the boys said, "We brought you some flowers." He was holding a beautiful bouquet of orange roses with pink carnations. I told them no one told me prom was happening today. I was hurt and a bit disappointed. It was understandable that it would be difficult as prom was not a time and place to be sad, but I had wanted to be there. I wanted to help decorate. I wanted to take photos. None of that happened.

Tucker's girlfriend whom he went to prom with just weeks before the accident was voted prom queen. Another of Tucker's best friends was prom king. His buddies, both girls and boys, were on the prom court. I couldn't help but think that Tucker may have been on court too. Even if he hadn't, it was a memorable evening that neither one of us took part in.

Tanner had been crowned prom king the year before at his junior prom. He would not attend and crown the new king since last year's queen was unable to join him that evening.

Later that day, I received a text from one of Tucker's best friends' mom letting me know they were thinking of me.

Graduation 2021

May 21, 2021. The graduates drove through town and walked through each of the schools to receive congratulatory messages from the elementary students and staff. Their last stop was in front of the village offices where the village clerk and I served them an ice cream sundae snack. We congratulated them and wished them well. I received hugs from some of the kids. The big day, graduation, would be tomorrow!

May 22, 2021, Graduation Day. Tucker visited me in a dream in the early morning. He was wearing his camouflage fleece shirt and talking up a storm. He seemed to be around age nine or ten, and I couldn't take my eyes off him.

It was Senior Graduation Day. The ceremony began at 2:00 p.m. At 1:15 p.m., four moms of Tucker's best friends showed up at our door with a beautiful bouquet of flowers. I gave them a group hug and told them this was a good day for all of us.

Dale, Tanner, and I arrived at the graduation ceremony, which took place outside, on the football field. It was preferred that large gatherings be held outside due to COVID. We propped up our lawn chairs behind everyone else. A number of people attending the ceremony approached us with little conversation said. Little needed to be said as many were thinking the same thoughts. Tucker's not here. On the bleachers, off to the side where the graduates sat, was a bouquet of white roses surrounding Tucker's photo. Emotions ran high. There were plenty of tears as the graduates came across the lawn and onto the stage. One graduate was missing. Our boy—dang! The valedictorian read his speech, acknowledging the absence of their classmate and touched on what this class had to endure throughout their high school years. Not only the loss of Tucker but having to wear mandatory masks with COVID-related mandates interrupting classes, after-school activities, clubs, and sports. These are times this group will never get back. As the graduates received their diplomas, the eight students who received Tucker's scholarship were also given a miniature eagle trophy. It was my understanding that this was the first time they knew who the recipients were who had been selected to receive the Tucker Westfall Scholarship. The salutatorian took the podium and gave her speech. The ceremony ended, and the graduates were instructed to go to their families sitting in their respective spots on the football field.

I watched as one of Tucker's best friends stopped briefly by his family on the football field. He then made a beeline toward me with the single white rose he had been given for the graduation ceremony. He reached out to give me the rose and burst into tears. I graciously accepted the rose and held him, not saying a word, just hugging and crying. There wasn't any more to say. It was quite an emotional moment. That hug, those tears, were all about Tucker. As I let go of my grasp on him, I glanced over to see Dale crying behind us. Tucker's friend went to him next.

Following closely behind was another of Tucker's friends. He wanted a hug as well and had eyes welled up with tears. Then he went to both Dale and Tanner giving them a hug.

Tucker Westfall Memorial Scholarship ($5,000)

2019 Graduation Day, May 18, 2019

First recipient. I was honored to be able to make the announcement in front of the graduates for the first Tucker Westfall Memorial Scholarship. This five thousand-dollar scholarship was awarded to Seth Coker. Seth had mentored Tucker on pitching for baseball and was an all-around top choice to receive this scholarship. He was named player of the year in baseball. Post-graduation plans were to head to University of La Crosse to major in mathematics and minor in business.

In February 2020, Wanda set up a website for the Tucker Westfall Memorial Scholarship to showcase the winners (www.westfallstrong.com). Tucker has a website in his name. Too much! So very special! Tanner says we don't need to advertise, saying, "Don't worry, the kids know about Tucker's scholarship!"

Second recipient, May 2020—Carter Brunke. Carter was Tucker's partner on the wrestling mat. He came to practices to help prepare Tucker for tournament time. Carter was a two-time WIAA state wrestling qualifier. Carter continued his wrestling career at the University of Wisconsin–Eau Claire. Unfortunately, due to a shoulder injury, his wrestling venture ended but has continued to concentrate on his studies in the business program.

Third recipients, May 2021. The scholarship was meant to be given to just one graduate each year, but it was optional, and this year an exception was made. All eight applicants who applied were in some way so deserving as each one of their scholarship applications shared a little piece of how Tucker touched their lives as well as how they touched Tucker's. It was a very special group of honorees.

Many photos of us with the scholarship recipients and graduates were taken after the graduation ceremony. What a special day! Congratulations to Tucker's classmates and scholarship winners: Jake Denzine, Dayne Diethelm, Cobie Ellenbecker, Michael Komarek, Autumn Westfall, Shauna Belter, Maleah Redmann, and Kaitlyn Riehle.

Fourth recipients, May 2022. Two recipients received Tucker's scholarship this year. Cooper Diedrich, the same friend who worked out in the weight room with Tucker in the bigger, faster, stronger program during middle school, not only is an honor roll student, but has flourished into an exceptional athlete in Athens' history, becoming player of the year in football, scoring over one thousand points and named player of the year two years in a row in basketball, and a standout shortstop and pitcher on the baseball field. Tucker knew he would be quite an athlete, saying, "Mom, he's going to be really good!" Well, he sure turned out that way and was just another "best friend" of Tucker's.

Siarra Hart is the other honoree. Recall, she hit a home run on the same day as the Tucker Westfall Field Dedication Ceremony and sports the number 12 on her softball jersey. Siarra is an honor roll student and has continued her successful high school softball career, being named First Team All-Conference. Recently, she became a licensed EMT. Since EMTs were so important in how they assisted Tucker, I hope she educates herself and returns to place down her roots locally so she, too, can be as influential to anyone requiring the same special care and medical help that was needed in Tucker's case.

TRACY WESTFALL

Westfall scholarship applications sought

Athens High School seniors graduating this spring of 2020, who plan to pursue a post-secondary education at an accredited technical college or university, are able to submit their applications for the Tucker Westfall Memorial $5,000 scholarship in the high school office from now until March 31, 2020. This scholarship was established in 2019 in memory of Tucker Westfall. Seth Coker was awarded the first Tucker Westfall Scholarship during the 2019 Athens High School graduation ceremony. Seth is currently pursuing a degree in mathematics education at UW-La Crosse. The scholarship award was also inscribed with Seth's name and will remain in the trophy case at Athens High School as a reminder of Seth's role in Tucker's life and Seth's own achievements as a superior role model. Pictured, from left to right, are Tracy Westall, Connor Westfall, Seth Coker with his scholarship trophy and Dale Westfall.

Seth Coker
Year 1

Carter Brunke
Year 2

HERE FOR A GOOD TIME, NOT A LONG TIME

8 Recipients/Classmates
Year 3

The Eight Recipients
From 2021

Cooper Diedrich And Siarra Hart With
The Westfall Family (Year 4)

Graduation 2021

CHAPTER 14

These Days

People still ask me for the T12 and T22 car stickers. One elderly lady in the village did not want to sell her car unless she received another Tucker sticker to replace the one she could not get off her car window. She was able to get another one from Grandma Engel.

Tucker's room has not changed. A few more memorable photos and books were added, like the photo of one of the 2021 Tucker Westfall Scholarship winner who took his photo kneeling next to Tucker's bust at the ball field, the senior photo autographed by each of his classmates, the senior football players sitting on a bench with Tucker shadowed in the background, and the Athens High School Annual dedicated in his honor. I continue to keep a current calendar in this room so we can talk about what season is coming up, how long he's been gone, and current events going on. He hears me.

In August 2019, I read *Do Dead People Watch You Shower?* by the medium Concetta Bertoldi. There are so many areas this author was on target with my experiences and beliefs. Near the end of the book, the author spoke about frogs coming around symbolizing a loved one. Isn't it interesting that I had pulled Tucker's little red frog from the garage sale box and placed it on the kitchen windowsill not long ago? I just was not going to sell it knowing baby frogs are a sign, and I'm sure he knows I kept that little red frog. I have seen quite a number of frogs recently, even mentioning it to Tanner one day.

The author also spoke about a *smile* being worthwhile. Right away my thoughts focused on Tucker's smile and what was written on the bronze legacy plaque in front of Tucker's bust at the ball field to greet each other with a smile.

In January 2021, I read *Imagine Heaven* by John Burke, who shared similar near-death experiences by numerous people. A simple philosophy and theme run throughout the book. God wants us to love all his children and all people. He does not care about your achievements, how much money you make, and the like on this earth. He cares most about how you have loved his children. That is why Tucker's in heaven. He cared. He put his own self aside to help others and was so kind to others. I understand now why he has that angel's wing and certainly is the type of young man who is deserving of the other. I understand why God would love to have him in his presence.

Our family runs in different directions these days. I try to keep my days full of acts of kindness in addition to continuing my work as an insurance adjuster. Slow times are bad for me, giving me too much time to think.

There was an opening on the Athens Village Board, so I considered it, filed the appropriate paperwork, ran for a trustee position, and was voted in for a two-year term. There is so much to do in our small village to help with current and future improvements that I felt the need to support those efforts.

One of the first things I did was purchase brackets for the street poles to hang petunia baskets to beautify the village over the summer months. This was something my sister Lorene and I had talked about doing several times, and I wanted to recognize my sister and Miltrim Farms for all they did in this little community. It was time for me to give back to the community for all they had done on behalf of our family and Tucker.

I cared for a dozen flower baskets like each was my own, getting up at 3:00 a.m., 4:00 a.m., or 5:00 a.m. in the mornings to water them with a handmade watering system I created. Other days, I went before sunset just to mix up the watering schedule a little. I don't sleep much anyway, so it kept me busy. The following year, I added to the dozen and purchased twelve more brackets and hanging flower baskets so they now can line a main street through Athens.

The village gazebo or "band shell" needed painting so I took on that job. It is the town centerpiece where the Old Timers Band would play on Friday nights during the summers. Imprinted on the concrete by the flagpole to the south of the band shell is a medallion in the shape of a large white circle highlighted with a blue ring. A white replica of the gazebo is pictured in the center highlighted in blue. The medallion circle is surrounded by three rows of bricks. The white and blue colors had faded over the years, so that got a coat of paint as well.

A one-way street with angled parking is on one side of the gazebo. This "main" street contains the grocery store, bakery, bowling alley, one of the local bars, and a few miscellaneous business offices. The street on the other side of the gazebo is Highway 97, which is the main thoroughfare leading from the north to the south through the village.

Just down the street from the gazebo is Veterans Memorial Park. The site has an army tank and flags, a covered open-air shelter, picnic tables, a few grills, and some playground equipment. I repainted the restrooms there and also the ones by the village softball fields. Any activity that would keep me busy and not at home crying was on the table. It was my way of healing.

In fall, I decided to purchase brightly colored baskets of mums to be placed with cornstalks around the village lampposts that lined the streets. Miltrim Farms donated the cornstalks, so Lorene, Tom, and I secured the cornstalks and mums to the lampposts for a nice fall decoration.

Dale and I purchased an old cargo van to haul aluminum cans. We take about an hour and a half every month to clear out the cage, sitting at a local gas station, which gets filled with bags of cans dropped off by people in the community. The proceeds are donated to the high school to support all high school athletics.

These are just a few of the little things that can make a difference and go a long way, as well as thanking all those in this little community who have given so much support to us. Tucker was a giver, and I wanted to focus on giving back in a number of useful ways. I want to join my guardian angel one day.

Dale is retired now from teaching and coaching but decided to work part-time two days a week at the local Maple Grove Charter School, a rural school about fifteen miles from town that was recently acquired by the Athens School District in July of 2021. He enjoys the extra spending cash to do what he wants.

Because of the retirement, Dale and I actually were able to watch our first Athens High School football game together on the bleachers on September 4, 2021. Dale was planning to retire after Tucker graduated from high school anyway, so I am glad he continued on with his plan. It was more like easing into retirement, though, with him taking on the part-time position at Maple Grove. He is also assisting with coaching wrestling and baseball. He just can't stay away from sports!

Tanner is attending the University of Stevens Point and paving his own path in life. He loves to hunt and fish, a family tradition he needs to carry on. I am very fortunate to have such a fine young son who has handled losing his brother in such a mature way.

Reflecting on what ifs happens often, wondering what Tucker would be like as a grown man. Would he have a girlfriend? What would his course of study be in college? Would he have gone to UW–Madison and played for the Badgers, or stayed local, attending a technical college and hanging with his buddies? I still talk to him every day and tell him I love him, cry before I go to bed, and again he is in my thoughts in the morning when I wake. Very vivid, detailed dreams still occur at night, not having figured out why. Restless nights continue, and although I may go to bed early, I wake up feeling like I haven't slept well. Going out socially and having a good time is hard to do as much as I would like to; the same empty feelings haunt me and likely will always be there. One can't hide them when they become a part of you, a part of what's missing and will always be missing. There is a feeling of hurt and brokenheartedness that just never goes away. Our lives have changed dramatically after losing Tucker, and we recognize that we will not get back what we had. Our lives are no longer what they were. The happiness and fulfillment of a complete family, sharing and enjoying our time together, is forever severed. We know it is gone and will never be back again and deal with it daily. This Westfall family is strong and continue to deal with change we'd never thought we would face.

*****

The Tucker Westfall Golf Outing is held annually at Black River Golf Course in Medford. My brother-in-law, Gary, manages the course. My youngest sister, Georgine, also helps volunteer at the course since her husband is there. She makes sure everything runs smoothly for the tournaments and sets up the raffle and drawing items. Many people donate special items for these outings.

Before the start of each tournament, there is a moment of silence in Tucker's honor, and special words are spoken in remembrance of him. The money raised in the past years has gone toward the baseball field renovation, football helmets, a batting cage, bats, wrestling backpacks, and other ongoing high school boys baseball, wrestling, and football needs. So much good has come from such a tragic situation. Alumni, farmers, family, friends, and many others involved in making Tucker Westfall Memorial Field what it has become still take part in the outings. It is a time to relax, golf, and enjoy each other's company.

At the first outing, Georgine and Gary had a special bald eagle memorial sign made in honor of Tucker for the golf course. For good reason, they wanted to place it at hole number 12, but it is only a nine-hole course. They didn't realize it, nor did I, until Dale reminded me that number 9 was his baseball uniform number. I had spent all those years washing his uniform and hanging it to dry, and it hadn't dawned on me the connection until Dale told me. Hole 9 was a perfect place for the dedication sign.

For the first annual golf tournament held in 2018, just months after the accident, special memorial T-shirts were made. One of Tucker's best friends came out to golf for the very first time. At hole 4, there was a prize for the longest putt, and he won. He said he hit it, and the ball kept rolling and rolling and fell in the hole. This best friend was in the UTV with Tucker when the accident occurred. I can't help but think Tucker helped on that putt! We raised over nineteen thousand dollars for the baseball field renovations at this first golf outing.

The second golf outing was going to be held to raise funds for the Athens football team. This was held on July 20, 2019, but strong winds, lightning, and rain had moved in minutes before the start of the tournament, forcing everyone inside the clubhouse. There was no golfing that day, but the many people who had showed up, stayed, ate, drank, and enjoyed each other's company. The raffles were held, and everyone sure looked like they had a good time. Four foursomes returned the following day when the weather cooperated to golf the course. Janelle Ewan selected number 22 for raffles, winning five raffles. Number 22 was Tucker's football number. That was an interesting coincidence for sure. About eleven thousand dollars was raised that day for the Athens football program.

We could not have a tournament in 2020 due to the pandemic, and the mandates restricted social gathering.

On July 24, 2021, the third golf outing for Tucker was held. It was a beautiful weather, and we had a full roster of golfers. Good times! "Ring of Fire" was played on the jukebox.

*****

Bald eagles still appear frequently, and blue jays hang out in the backyard. I feel Tucker is always near, and he continues to give me signs.

I spend a lot of time in the woods hunting deer. I call it T time.

Dale and I still go to Tucker Westfall Memorial Field just to be there. It is a special place for us and a reflection of what his classmates, friends, school, and community meant to him and did for us. How do you ever give back enough to everyone to show how grateful our family is?

I realize many others are out there going through losses of their own children or loved ones. The grief symptoms are handled so differently by each. I wanted to share my story because Tucker, and what has happened in this community as a result of his death, is such an inspirational story that needed to be shared. One is not alone when a loss of a significant person in your life occurs. Tucker is close; however, I wish I could see him, touch him, talk to him directly, but knowing his spirit and love are right in our home is the best any mom could ever want from their own child. He has made this very clear to me, and I love him for it. It helps me deal with the pain and heartache I struggle with daily. The good Lord challenges us in many ways, testing us with the very lows and enjoying the very highs of life. I believe how we give to others here on earth follows through upon our passing. I live now with this understanding more and more each day. Complaining and petty little issues have little meaning and serve no value. How we treat others, and how we are received by others, is far more important in the eyes of the Lord.

I still run into Tucker's friends occasionally. They have spread out now that high school is over, but several of them still hang out together. We have bonded in a very special way after all that we have shared in the past few years. They each hold a special place in my heart.

The Autumn Blaze maple and two-toned maple trees received as memorial gifts from the funeral are in our backyard. They continue to grow taller and flourish every year. The vibrant fall colors of the trees enhance the ambiance and serenity of the firepit. The firepit area will always be a sanctuary for us. It is a daily reminder for me as I look out my office window upstairs and the kitchen window on the first floor of Tucker's last request that he was able to enjoy one special time.

HERE FOR A GOOD TIME, NOT A LONG TIME

TRACY WESTFALL

Village Flower Baskets For Lorene/Miltrim Farms

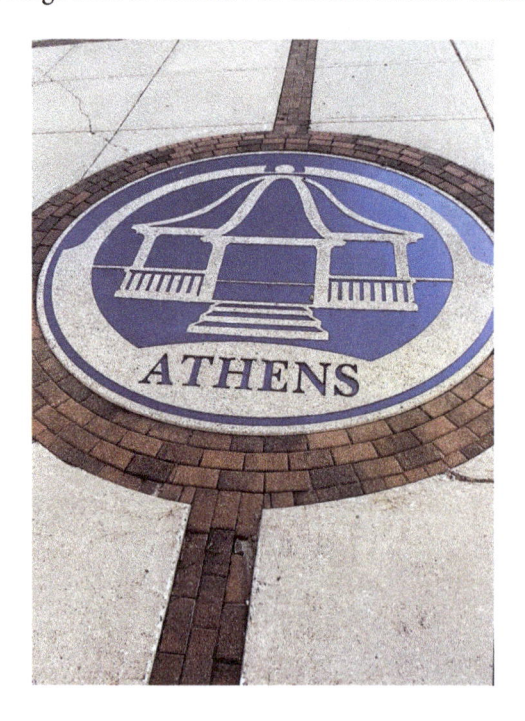

HERE FOR A GOOD TIME, NOT A LONG TIME

Downtown Gazebo Athens

Tanner, Tracy, Georgine, Lorene, & Steve (Brother)

Par 9 In Memory Of Tucker
Black River Golf Course
Medford, WI

HERE FOR A GOOD TIME, NOT A LONG TIME

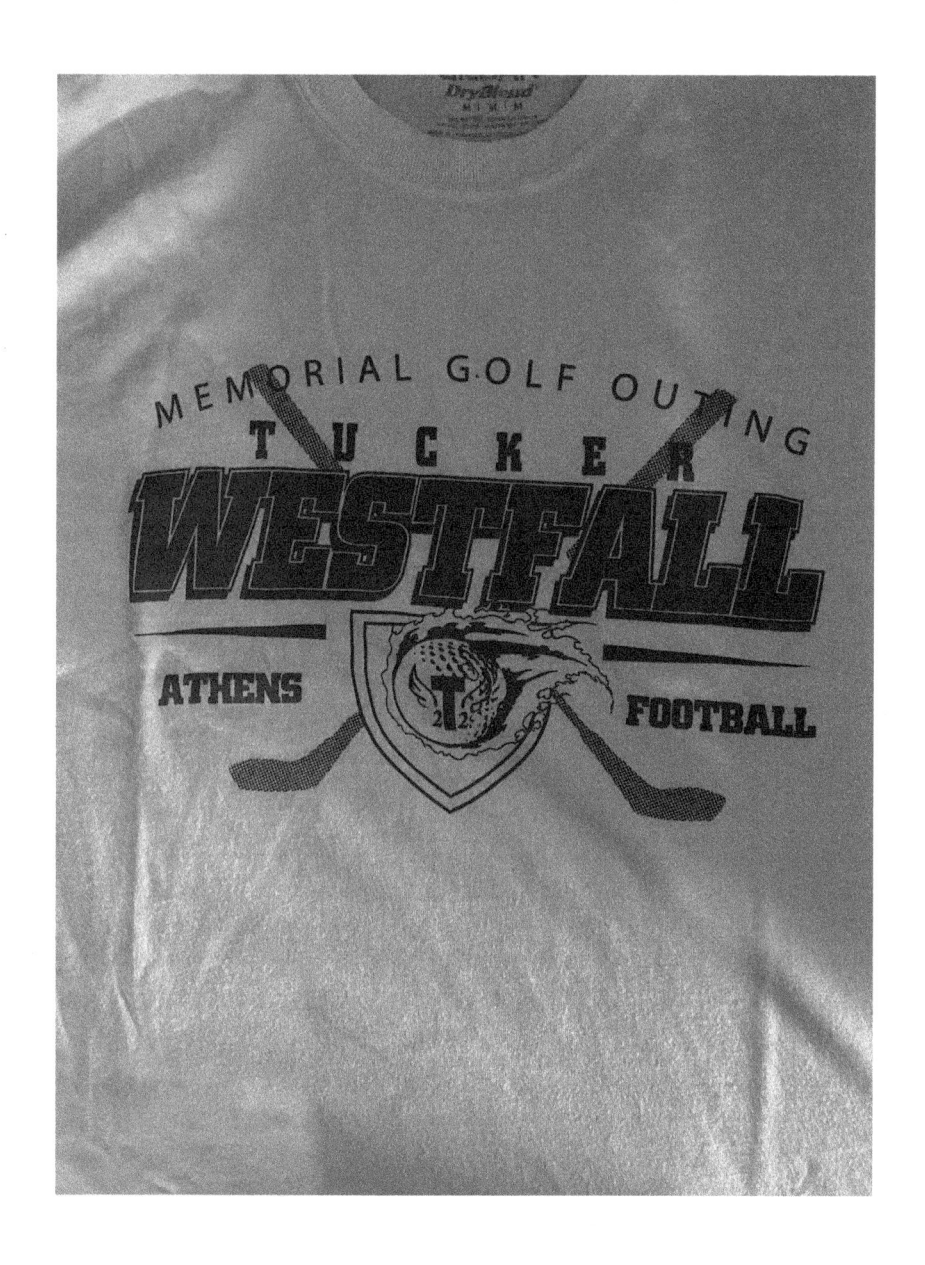

CHAPTER 15

My Guardian Angel

This book now ends in the final way I can honor Tucker. Tucker has shown me, and others, in so many ways he is near. I have not ignored the signs but embraced them. Our community has honored him in ways most would only dream of. Every being in me senses that he knows this and appreciates what was done for him, and I am sure he would love to thank so many. The books I have referenced convince me that I am not alone in my grief in losing a loved one but that I am the fortunate one to have gained a guardian angel for the rest of my lifetime.

My shared experiences are unique, so you should draw your own conclusions. This book was prepared from my viewpoint of my time with Tucker. I do hope I got the stories and facts from others to me correctly. We lost a real fine young man who is loved and missed daily. His loss impacted this community and our lives on earth forever, but he has also strengthened and made believers in many of us through his actions after life. Our family has felt warmth, comfort, and support from so many, and we thank you. Realize one cannot take even a day for granted, as every day here on earth counts because tomorrow may not come. Not a day goes by where I do not have thoughts of him, wonder about what could have been, where he would be today, and all the good times we should be sharing. Yes, all the good times. Tucker said it best, "We are all here for a good time!" In his case, "not a long time."

HERE FOR A GOOD TIME, NOT A LONG TIME

The words I had written shortly after Tucker's passing, which I wanted in a song, is instead a poem helping me to heal.

Fly High

It was a cloudy day that early June morn
Mom dropped the boys at uncle tom's farm to
Pick rocks in the field for next year's corn
Something went wrong which changed all of their lives
As they headed out on that graveled road
The UTV veered right and the unit rolled
His two buddies with him came out all right
But tucker, tucker's not coming home tonight

Many family members and friends gathered at the school
The pastor gave prayer and the entire community was moved
By the death of a young man who had just started to bloom

TRACY WESTFALL

His favorite song was Johnny Cash's "Ring of Fire"
He wanted this played when he married some summer.
The bald eagle collection he cherished at home
Is now a symbol of love to all who have known

So fly high, young man
Soar like an eagle
We know you're in heaven
Though your loss we still feel
We're all down here; we're trying to heal

He's blessed us down here, to those who have known him.
But for his mom he was so close to, it's taken its toll
The loss of her son and the change of her role
So many say that she is so strong
But night after night she cries herself to sleep
Saying how could this have gone so wrong

It's another day without him
She asks, "what am I to do?"
Her heart is so broken
As much of her world revolved around you
The picture can't talk as she stares at the wall
She can't hear him walking side by side with her in the fall
She wishes she never lost him this way
A part of her is dying every day

Fly high, young man
Soar like an eagle
She knows you're in heaven
Though your loss she still feels
Son, just know mom's down here; she's trying to heal

It's the smell of his hat
And the presence in his room
Although there's a deep sense of loss

HERE FOR A GOOD TIME, NOT A LONG TIME

This helps carry her through
And oh, she's looking for his signs
So many can relate to what she's going through
As someone died that they were close to too
Together they share, it gives them something to hold on to
We all need each other to carry us through

So fly high, young man
Soar like an eagle
We're all coming together; we're all trying to heal

Now as we watch his classmates grow
The balloon release, the planted tree—
what a great bunch he had known
And, yet thankful too, that they have
experienced his kindhearted soul
He knows about the baseball field wishing
he could express how he feels
You know he shines above us at our
hometown football field
And his jersey and eagle displayed above
the high school gym door
Are just pleasant reminders of what our hearts hold dear.
Fly high, young Tucker, we know you are here

Fly high, young man
Soar like an eagle
We are thinking of you; we are beginning to heal

As the years pass by
Only the memories remain
The heart remains broken
And the pain…well, the pain just never goes away
Only to know we will be with you some day

TRACY WESTFALL

So fly high, young man
Soar like an eagle
We still think of you—as we continue to heal

fly high, tucker...we love you!

A FRIENDLY TRIBUTE TO TUCKER

Sentiments from Tucker's friends were made into a special book presented to me on June 2, 2021. I'm sharing them with you.

    I don't remember a lot with Tucker, but all the memories I do are all good ones. I remember a game we would always play in Elementary School was Tackle Tucker. It was a difficult game. I also recall that we always made Nelly mad in physical science when we played Kahoot. We would sit in front of her desk or beside it and ask which one is right. Also, I remember Tucker asking if I was going to go out for wrestling so I can be his dummy bag to practice on. I would always consider it because I could literally fight my best friend fair and square. I really will cherish every memory from Tucker I have. Fly high Tuck, fly high!

—Alex Mengel

    I remember one time when Kaden, Tucker, Schmood, Joy and I went kayaking and there was a tree down in the way and we had to go over it. Tucker went flying over it, fell off, and lost both of his crocs. He wasn't too mad because he ordered new ones that came in the next day.

—Brody Lipinski

Tucker was one of the most positive, funny, happy, and kind-hearted people I've ever known. I don't remember a time when he wasn't smiling or laughing. He was one of my best friends, and he was like a brother to me. We had a lot of good times together. Whether it was in school, sports, or just hanging out, he always seemed to brighten my mood. I remember throwing passes to him in middle school football, playing catch with him in baseball and sitting next to and goofing around with him in Mrs. Nelson's class. Those are only a few of the countless memories I made with Tucker. There's not a day that goes by where I don't think about Tuck, and it feels as if there is a piece of me missing.

—Cobie Ellenbecker

I lost my best friend during this sports season. Every time I step on the field it reminds me of him and all of our memories with each other. There isn't one day I don't think about him.

—Dayne Diethelm

Some of my best memories that I have of Tucker came when he would show up to my house without letting me know. It only happened a couple of times, but they always seemed to be our best times together.

—Jacob Brumbaugh

I will never forget the day Tucker and I were biking around town hiding from our other friends. We were just sitting there talking, calling them, telling them we were at a different place.

We had a lot of great memories, and I wish we could have had many more. Miss you buddy!

—Jake Denzine

I have quite a few memories of Tucker growing up. One of my favorites was one particular summer. I would bike down to Tucker's house nearly every day. We would play in the woods behind their house a lot and flag football was also a common activity in the backyard. We would shoot basketball in the driveway and Tucker and Tanner would always beat me in the game around the world. One of our favorite games we played was called "Tackle Tucker," which was pretty much a challenge for us rather than Tucker himself. He would run the football from one end of the yard to the other and Dakota, Tanner and I would try to tackle him before he reached the other side.

—Kaden Redmann

Being in almost every class with Tucker sometimes only a group of six of us, I got to know Tucker really well. Whether it was gym or health, he always knew how to put a smile on my face and give everyone a good laugh. There was always an inside joke that had us cracking up for days. When a good friend was taken from us, a piece of our hearts went with it and he will be forever remembered.

—Kaitlyn Riehle

Some of my best memories with Tucker were swimming down by Autumn's house in the creek. He was always the first one in the water.

Anytime we were bored we were down by the creek swimming. We had so much fun.

—Kyle Peel

One of my favorite memories with Tucker is when we were in study hall we would play Fortnite the whole time with Jake. We would also work ahead in math and play during class. We would always argue who was the best and just played all class period.

—Michael Komarek

A memory I have with Tucker is picking rock the Spring before the accident. It was just me and him picking rock talking about all the things we'd do once we got out of high school. The week before his accident we were having a conversation about what we wanted our senior quote to be. Tucker told me he wanted his to be, "We are here for a good time, not a long time."

—Patrick Redmann

Tucker was such a light in everyone's life. Two memories I will cherish forever would be going to the prom with him. It was so fun and I'm glad I was able to experience my first prom with him. Another would be having Spanish class with him our freshman year where he made the whole class laugh every single day just by making one goofy joke. I know we all miss him a lot and will keep him in our thoughts and prayers forever.

—Shauna Belter

Tucker was not only one of my many cousins, but one of my best friends too and that's something I will forever keep close to my heart. He was always the one person I knew I could go to when I needed a laugh and not worry about anything else going on. There simply is nobody like him. I have so many wonderful memories with him, it's hard to pick out just one to share. One of my favorites though is our freshman year, on a very warm day. We obviously were too young to drive yet so it came down to us deciding to go swimming in the Black Creek. Which was very convenient for Tucker and I because we both live right by it. If anybody knows what that creek is like, you know it's a little crazy for us to be swimming in there. For us though, it didn't matter, we were all together, no worries in the world and just simply having a good time. Words cannot explain how much I miss making new memories with Tuck. Every time we all get together, he's always in my mind and wishing he was physically there with us. Not a day goes by that I don't think about him but I know he's forever going to continue living on through us all. I miss him more and more every single day but I don't think I could ask for a better guardian angel to watch over me and all of us here.

—Autumn Westfall

These sentiments are from his friends/classmates. Tucker touched so many others including family, schoolmates, teammates, teachers, and community members.

There is a separate page in white bold print in a black background that reads:

> Always remember that "those we love don't go away; they walk beside us every day, unseen, unheard, but always near, still loved, still missed, still very dear." (author unknown)

ACKNOWLEDGEMENTS

Special thanks to those who supported me to write a book, my sister Wanda, who assisted in editing, and to that very special editor mom who provided the guidance I needed.

Thank you to the many kind and caring family members and friends who helped our family get through losing Tucker. Sometimes not saying a word but just being there was enough. Sometimes the smile from a distance or the soft hug meant so much. The many specially created symbolic memorial items and trinkets are cherished and remain displayed in our home.

APPENDIX A

Many thanks to all those who made Tucker Westfall Memorial Field.

Miltrim Farms, Inc.
S.D. Ellenbecker, Inc.
Janke General Contractors, Inc.
Switlick & Sons, Inc.
Kafka Granite, LLC
Peter Trucking, LLC
Jahnke Construction
Martin Wiese Electric
Cropping Central, LLC
Complete Crete, LLC
Rib Falls Repair
Black Rock Ready Mix, LLC
Kyle Switlick
Al Hopperdietzel
Glen Kafka
Athens Hardware
Bob Liss
VFW/American Legion
Terry Ball
Athens Alumni
Athens Fire Department
Albrecht Family Farms
Frahm Wood Products, Inc.
Events, Inc.
The Granite Shop, LLC
Tucker's Memorial Fund

TRACY WESTFALL

Bill Ellenbecker
Willy Rietz
Bill Yessa
Mike Wolf
Tom Ellenbecker
Andy Johnson
Athens School District
Many volunteers and students and friends

CPSIA information can be obtained
at www.ICGtesting.com
Printed in the USA
BVHW091003160523
664251BV00021B/654

9 798886 444636